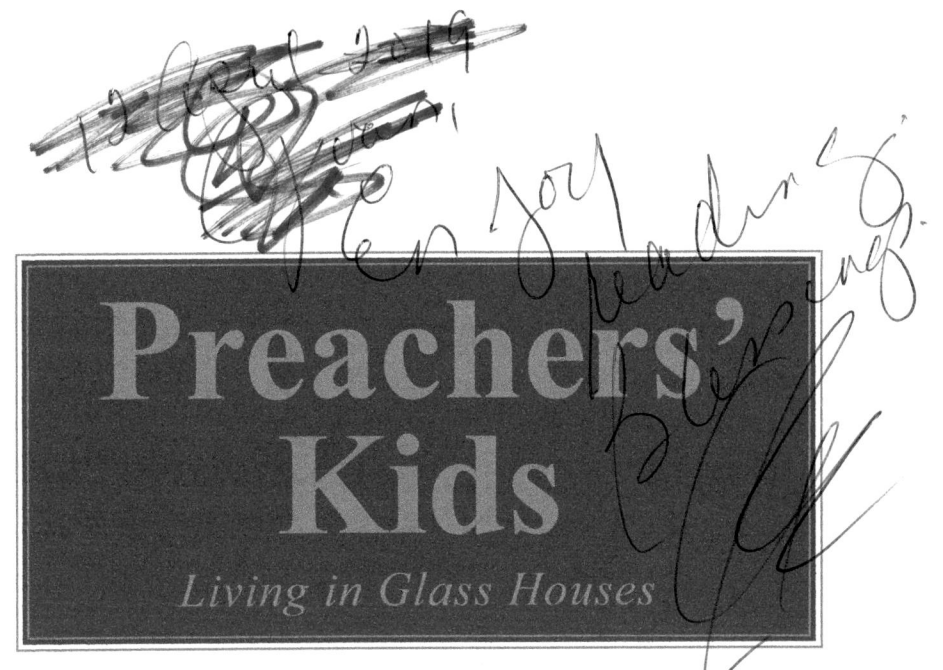

Preachers' Kids
Living in Glass Houses

Rev. Dr. Arnetha Bowens

Copyright © 2017 Arnetha Bowens.

All rights reserved. No part of this book may be used or reproduced by any means, graphic, electronic, or mechanical, including photocopying, recording, taping or by any information storage retrieval system without the written permission of the author except in the case of brief quotations embodied in critical articles and reviews.

Scripture taken from the King James Version of the Bible.
Scripture taken from the *Amplified Bible*, copyright © 1954, 1958, 1962, 1964, 1965, 1987 by The Lockman Foundation. Used by permission.

All Scripture quotations in this publications are from The Message. Copyright © by Eugene H. Peterson 1993, 1994, 1995, 1996, 2000, 2001, 2002. Used by permission of NavPress Publishing Group.

WestBow Press books may be ordered through booksellers or by contacting:

WestBow Press
A Division of Thomas Nelson & Zondervan
1663 Liberty Drive
Bloomington, IN 47403
www.westbowpress.com
1 (866) 928-1240

Because of the dynamic nature of the Internet, any web addresses or links contained in this book may have changed since publication and may no longer be valid. The views expressed in this work are solely those of the author and do not necessarily reflect the views of the publisher, and the publisher hereby disclaims any responsibility for them.

Any people depicted in stock imagery provided by Thinkstock are models, and such images are being used for illustrative purposes only.
Certain stock imagery © Thinkstock.

ISBN: 978-1-5127-3920-6 (sc)
ISBN: 978-1-5127-3921-3 (hc)
ISBN: 978-1-5127-3919-0 (e)

Library of Congress Control Number: 2016921578

Print information available on the last page.

WestBow Press rev. date: 12/19/2016

Dedication

Dedicated in loving memory to my dear righteous parents: Bishop George Law Bowens, Jr. and Mother Mary Ruth Bowens, with fond memories. Thank you both for rearing my siblings and me as you did. Your children and grandchildren call you both blessed. Again, thank you, and may God always bless your posterity. Your loving kindness, care and concern for all of us will always be appreciated, remembered, and cherished.

This book is also dedicated to The Children of The Reverend Clergy. In particular, to the late Missionary Nesta Washington. [May God Bless Her Memory.]

Again, this book is written to and for all Preachers' Kids, and the Children of Those Who Serve: "Living in Glass Houses" while feeling trapped, even cornered without knowing how to find their way out. Pks, this Book is for you!!

"Feeding the Hungry Souls Outreach Ministry for Christ"

"Help Is On The Way"

"Tomorrow, before the sun goes down, you shall have help."

*An Encouragement Sermon
Preached by my Dad,*
Bishop George Law Bowens, Jr.

Bible Text: II Kings 7:1-20

"Feed The Hungry Souls"

*Parents' Ministry Outreach Mission:
Taught by my Mom,*
Mother Mary Ruth Bowens

"For I was an hungred, and ye gave Me meat:
I was thirsty, and ye gave Me drink:
I was a stranger, and ye took me in:
Naked, and ye clothed Me:
I was sick, and ye visited Me:
I was in prison, and ye came unto me."

Bible Text: Matthew 25:35-36

WELCOME

This Book belongs to:

_____

                                      Date: _____

Gift given by: _____

                                      Date: _____

Comments: _____

_____

_____

_____

"The blessing of the LORD, it maketh rich, and He addeth no sorrow with it." (Proverbs 10:22)

"O TASTE AND SEE THAT THE LORD IS GOOD: BLESSED IS THE MAN THAT TRUSTETH IN HIM."

Psalm 34:8

Table of Contents

Dedication	iii
"Feeding the Hungry Souls Outreach Ministry for Christ"	iv
Bishop George Law Bowens, Jr.	
"Help Is On The Way"	iv
Mother Mary Ruth Bowens	
"Feed The Hungry Souls"	iv
Welcome	v
Acknowledgments	xi
A Time to Say Thanks	xi
A Prayer of Thanks	xii
Preface	xiii
Chapter 1. Our Only Wish Is To Be Normal	1
Chapter 2. Accept Me For Me!!! Let Me Be Me!!!	5
Lives Ending In Tragedy	6
Another Story	7
Chapter 3. How Do You See Yourself?	9
Let's Talk	10
Chapter 4. The Worst Kind of What?	13
Chapter 5. Forgive The Offenders	19
Example	20
Chapter 6. "To Every Thing There Is A Season"	25
Chapter 7. Be Aware of Hindrances	31
Be Watchful	33
Chapter 8. Discovering Your Enemy	37

	Words Have Power 38
	Make A Fresh Start 39
	Prayers for Deliverance and Salvation 40
Chapter 9.	Preachers' Kids, Let's Talk..43
	Examples of The Potency of "I AM" 45
	Stop Trying to Please Man 45
	You Are A King's Kid..47
	Plant Righteous Seeds 48
Chapter 10.	How Committed Are You? 51
	Restoration..53
Chapter 11.	Reflections: In Retrospect 55
	Midway Musings 55
	Did You know?... 58
	A Prologue: Mother Mary Ruth Bowens........................... 62
	Dealing with Peers 62
	Question & Answer 62
	Words of Wisdom: My Mom.. 62
	Scriptures for Meditation 63
Chapter 12.	The ISness of God 69
	Fruit of the Spirit 74
Chapter 13.	The Call of God 75
Chapter 14.	The Zealous Clergy 81
	The Spouse 83
Chapter 15.	Who Are These People? 89
	Face YOUR Hurts 90
	The Vision 93

Chapter 16.	Watch Fanaticism	95
	Reality Check	96
	Example	101
Chapter 17.	You Are In Need of A Healing	103
Chapter 18.	The Life of Preachers' Kids	107
	Example	107
	Example	110
	Scriptures to Encourage	112
	Prayer	114
Chapter 19.	Children of The Reverend Clergy	115
	Let Me Encourage You With These Words	115
	Opines from An Anesthetizer	116
Chapter 20.	From This Day Forth	119
	No More Excuses	119
Chapter 21.	Words of Encouragement: Bishop Joseph P. Bowens	121
	Change Your Thoughts	121
Chapter 22.	Epilogue: Merging the Trek	123
	In Summary	123
	ASK: The Key to Answered Prayer	134

A Useful Study Reference	135
An Offering Unto the LORD	141
The Benediction	141
"May the Lord Bless You"	142
Contact Information	143
Coming Soon: Other Inspirational Books!	144
About the Author	145

Note: Initial Caps are intentionally used for such words as: Bishop, Children, Church, Citizen, Dad, Mom, Glass House, Ministry, Offspring, Parent(s) Pastor, Preachers' Kids, Priest, Public Servants, Royalty, Synagogue, The Reverend Clergy and the like; aimed at an emphatic effect

Acknowledgments

A Time to Say Thanks . . .

Special thanks to my dynamic siblings: Bishop/Pastor Joseph P. Bowens; Missionary Helen Gray; Minister James R. Bowens, Sr.; Bernice Oakman, BSN, and Martie Martin, Education and Business Advocate. I have been truly blessed by your love, prayers and support. Your words of encouragement are highly valued. I have learned so much from all of you. Much love to the blessed memory of my sister, Missionary Margaret Hardeman and my brother, Evangelist David Bowens, Sr. You are the very best family anyone could ever have. I love and appreciate each and every one of you, for being you. Thanks for loving me, for me, with all of my idiosyncrasies.

Affectionate enjoyment and appreciation to my fervent prayer support team: Abigail Hurley and Dominic Hurley, II. *"But Jesus said, Suffer little children, and forbid them not, to come unto me: for of such is the kingdom of heaven."* (Matthew 19:14)

Loving gratitude to my faithful Prayer Partners: Mrs. Ellen Bowens, Minister Lynne Galloway, Missionary Helen Gray, Pastor Linda Grissett, Minister Vera Hawley Groce, Evangelist Elizabeth Hutchings, Missionary Dollie Diane Taylor and Dr. & Mrs. Joseph L. Ross, Sr. You are a God-sent blessing and a vital inspired fellowship to me. Thanks for being in prayer for and with me, while I worked on this book.

Special thanks to my nieces and nephews: Jeanette Hardeman, Joy Hurley, David L. Bowens, Jr., Gerald A. Martin, Jr. and Gerome Martin.

Sincere appreciation to Mr. Charles Lanier, and Ms. Marsha Stroman, for their noteworthy contributions in helping me get my book published.

Thanks to everyone who shared precious ingredients of their life stories. They reminisced and mused over the good, the awful, the unattractive and the better, while growing up as Preachers' Kids; also known as Children of The Reverend Clergy. Evangelist Maudesta Claiborne, Ms. Sylvia Davis, Missionary Helen Gray, Missionary Joy Hurley, Ms. Sylvia Long, Ms. Carolyn Mole, Mrs. Tracey Pryce and The Reverend Janice Roberts. Thank You! Your heartwarming "Words of Wisdom" will help encourage other Pk members of this select alliance. Words cannot express my sincere gratitude to all of you.

Grateful appreciation to Martie for believing in me, and helping me put this baby to bed [print language for getting this book published]. Again, thank you.

Finally, my heartfelt thanks to Bishop Joseph P. Bowens for his prayers, and special "Words of Encouragement." He always reminds us to: "Let God Arise" in every facet of our lives.

> *"Let God arise, let His enemies be scattered: let them also that hate Him flee before Him."*
> —Psalm 68:1

A Prayer of Thanks

Father God, You are awesome! You heard and answered my prayer. Thank You, Lord, for all You have done, are doing and will continue doing for me. I love, honor and adore You. Use this book offering for Your glory to make a difference across America, and around the world in the lives of men, women, boys and girls. Amen. Amen.

> *"O magnify the Lord with me, and let us exalt His Name together."*
>
> —Psalm 34:3

Preface

This book is written to and for the Children of The Reverend Clergy, as well as the Children of all Public Servants. These service providers, in an effort to make a difference for others, have likewise, dedicated their lives to the benefit, well-being, safety and security of humanity. This exemplary group are daily serving us. They are professionally doing their jobs as Public Servants. These amazing Citizens are willing to respond to human need, at any moment, at any happening, oftentimes putting their own lives at risk.

In spite of everything, many who serve, may come from humble beginnings and have very little wealth. Nonetheless, they give their lives to the call of God; to Minister and care for the need of others. These extraordinary people come from all religions, faiths and denominations. As one, they are collectively recognized, as The Reverend Clergy. This is the purpose for which this book was written. Together, all of these Children are tucked-in under an ageless, giant alliance umbrella, termed "Preachers' Kids." We are indebted to all of them [all of us] both religious and secular. Pain hurts, no matter the cause, or the situation. Hence, we offer all of you [all of us] an eternal: *"We Love You."*

Over and over again, Children of The Reverend Clergy, as well as family members, are repeatedly, referred to as:

- Bench warmer
- Church-goer
- Fault finder
- Goody-goody
- Goody two-shoes
- Grundy
- Holier-than-thou

- Holy Joe
- Nice Nelly
- Self-righteous
- Rabbis Kids
- PKs
- Politicos' Kids
- Preachers' Kids
- Puritan
- Wowser.

On occasion, the name calling and taunting seem endless. Countless cruel acts, and unkind hurtful words are hurled toward innocent Children, simply due to the occupations of their Parents, and/or family members. Accordingly, Children of Athletes and Entertainers may experience the same kind of intimidation and spitefulness.

Perhaps, you were born into a religious family? Maybe, you were adopted by a political family? Perchance, you were given to a family in professional sport, as a foster child? No matter the situation; it was by no fault of your own. You played no part in the decision-making. Although we have no choice in its' membership; it does not matter. The PK alliance is perpetual; consisting of all peoples, cultures and customs. It is ageless, color-blind and global.

This book is for you. This book is for me. It is written to you. It is written to me. It attempts to address issues, problems and situations that challenge all of us. I know you have questions about your family member's call to help others; while your family may need a little consideration. Some of your conflicts, [our conflicts] may have resided in and with you [us] since childhood. These uncertainties may include unresolved struggles ranging from: who we are, to what is the purpose of our life. You may wonder how I know? Very simply, I am, like many of you – A Preachers' Kid.

Enjoy,

Rev. Dr. Arnetha Bowens

Our Only Wish Is To Be Normal

Chapter 1

We are Children of The Reverend Clergy. A member of our family may be a Cleric, a Nun, a Deacon, an Elder, a Mother of the Church, or perhaps a Choir member. You see, our alliance is all-embracing extensive, inclusive, distinctive and influential. There are no external features, nor internal attributes that can separate us. We come in all ages, sizes, professions, cultures, class and ethnicity,. We are all together. We are one. We all share the same 'PK' pigeonhole. It doesn't matter the color of our eyes; how much we look like Uncle; the hue of our skin; where we live; how high we can jump; nor the amount of sinful acts we participate in, or involve ourselves; we are all marked – PK! Our only brand is and always will be: "Preachers' Kids." All of us, collectively, have been and always will be seared with an ageless hot iron, PKs: "One of them." "So you think you're so much – *the Holy Ones.* We'll show you!"

Remember the story of Peter's denial of his dear friend, Jesus. Until then, he appeared to be a loyal and faithful Disciple of Jesus. Yet, in the end, he could not break away from his prior allegiance to Jesus and his fellow Apostles. No matter how Peter, "often looked up to as a Rock," tried to obscure himself, he could not escape the scrutiny of being discovered: "One of Them!!"

Luke 22:54c-60a writes about a man in conflict with his own faith. When faced with his acclaimed religious conviction, this close friend of Jesus, 'wish at heart', was to fade away into the crowd. It reads: *"And Peter followed afar off. And when they had kindled a fire in the midst of the hall, and were set down together, Peter sat down among them. But a certain maid beheld him as he sat by the fire, and earnestly looked upon him, and said, This man was also with Him. And he denied Him, saying, Woman, I know Him not. And after a little while another saw him, and said, Thou art also of them. And Peter said, Man, I am not. And about the space of one hour after another confidently affirmed, saying, Of a truth this fellow also was with Him: for he is a Galilaean. And Peter said, Man, I know not what thou sayest."*

As Preachers' Kids, how often, do we follow our Parents, and/or family members from afar? Sometimes, people may recognize us, and ask: "Don't I know you?" Frequently, the reply is, "I don't think so." Not convinced, they may say: "Yes, you are the Pastor's child." We may respond, "I don't know what you are talking about. Everyone has a twin." Our intent was not to deceive her. We simply didn't validate her speculation. Returning home, we are met head-on with: "Why did you mislead that dear Lady?" Be aware, there is always a 'duty' Hotline to PKs' families. Before arriving back home, our Parents would receive telephone calls, as to where we were, who we were with, and address our behavior.

The PK brand belongs to the Children of those who work to make the quality of life better and easier for others. Our Parents, and family members are those who serve in every area of life, sharing of themselves and making improvements wherever they can. It does not matter what their titles are, we have one thing in common. We are the Children of those who contribute their lives to service. Our Parents and families are those on the front line, always on display, always on call. Year-in, year-out, month-in, month-out, day-by-day, throughout all seasons, life cycles, ceremonies, sacraments, life struggles, sorrows, joys and celebrations; The Reverend Clergy usually serve for their entire lives. Their vocations spread far and wide across all nations, cultures, nationalities, traditions, religious affiliations and into all the world. These Holy men and women serve as Pastors, Bishops, Elders, Evangelists, Nuns, Teachers, Rabbis, Cantors, Rectors, Chaplains, Ambassadors, Counselors, Missionaries, Ministers, Prophets, Priests and Inspirational Leaders. Their Cleric duties consist of, but are not limited to:

- Always Praying
- Baptisms
- Births
- Blessings
- Charity
- Christenings
- Counseling

- Daycare
- Education
- Fasting
- Feeding the Hungry
- Fundraising
- Funerals
- Holiday Celebrations
- Holy Days' Observances
- Hospitality
- Preaching
- Sacraments
- Sermonize
- Visiting the Prisons
- Visiting the Sick
- Weddings, and so on
- Praying Continually.

As a result, here we are the family and Children of The Reverend Clergy. Frequently, we never get to really know them. Nonetheless, as their Children, we were born to live in *Glass Houses* with them. Our directives are to live righteous, supportive, exemplary lives; always cognizant that we are PKs. A family member of The Reverend Clergy told me, that their three Children only had two public requirements.

The first essential can been seen in a reflection from Proverbs 22:1: *"A GOOD name is rather to be chosen than great riches, and loving favour rather than silver and gold."* The Children were told: "Keep our name clean." The second essential is a prayer from Psalm 25:2. *"O my God, I trust in Thee: let me not be ashamed, let not mine enemies triumph over me."* The Children were told that they could party hardy like they just didn't care; but while they were at it, they were advised: "Don't make us ashamed." Today, they are all adults. Yet, these essential specifics are forever branded onto their souls and in their conscience.

"LET THE WORDS OF MY MOUTH, AND THE MEDITATION OF MY HEART, BE ACCEPTABLE IN THY SIGHT, O LORD, MY STRENGTH, AND MY REDEEMER."

Psalm 19:14

Accept Me For Me!!! Let Me Be Me!!!

Chapter 2

We are Children of The Reverend Clergy. Please, allow me to let you in on a little secret. Our lives and the lives of our families are continuously examined and scrutinized. We hurt. We loose hope. We wish for, and want love and acceptance. We want to be celebrated; not tolerated. As quiet as it is kept, at times, we look for love in all the wrong places. The same desire may be true for many of you. When we get discouraged, it eats at the very core of our being. We sometimes become like the prodigal son who squandered his inheritance on riotous living. After sowing our wild oats, we often get angry with ourselves. We blame God. We blame our Parents. We blame other people. We blame John Q Public. We even blame the Church, rather than taking responsibility for our own mistakes. The Children of 'Those Who Serve' want acceptance for who we are, and *NOT* for who, and what our Parents are. We have flesh on our bones, and blood running warm in our veins; the same as all of you. Our basic human needs are the same as the next person: food, clothing and shelter. Nonetheless, most of all, we desire love, kindness and respect.

People tend not to let us be on our own. They want us to become replicas of our Parent[s], Grandparents and/or Guardians. We are likely to be 'off-ended' by their 'fishing' platitudes all the time. For example, why are you not like your parents? Why are you not helping more in Ministry with your Parents? Are you really saved? Do you know Jesus? Your Parents need you to help them in the Ministry. People want to believe that Children of The Reverend Clergy were born into Ministry to Minister. This experience is comparable for most of the Children in the PK alliance.

Our spirits cry out, we are individuals, not Preachers, nor Deacons nor Choir members. We are Children of The Reverend Clergy. Our sobs and whimpers [often silent] is ACCEPT ME FOR ME!! Accept Us! Let ME Be ME!!! Please allow me to pursue my personal dreams and aspiration, not yours, nor theirs. Are you willing to permit me to reach for my desired vision? I have something to offer humanity. I have special gifts, talents and abilities. Let me off your predetermined merry-go-round, to search for my explicit life work. LISTEN to me!!! I have something to say. STOP comparing me to my parents, and/or my grandparents. Stop comparing me to my brothers, sisters, and/or cousins! STOP comparing me with other peoples' Kids. Most of all, please STOP comparing me with and to your Kids.

STOP! LOOK! LISTEN! LOOK AT ME NOW. I AM an individual. As quiet as it is kept, God has given me brilliance, personality and amazing skills. I am grateful that God bequest wisdom, knowledge and understanding into my life. Listen to what I have to say. I want to be heard. I am not a clone of my Parents nor my Grandparents. I am an individual. I love life and want to find my way. I desire to fulfill the intentions of my heart. Please, do not hinder me from reaching my destiny. God is ordering my steps. Stop throwing hindrances of any kind in my path. I am jaded from *Living In A Glass House*. Please, give me some privacy. Allow me to interact with other people, without constant snooping, analysis, criticism, and/or exploratory reviews. If you refuse to help me; please do not hinder, nor obstruct my progress.

Lives Ending In Tragedy

I heard this story a few years ago. The son of a Pastor went to Vietnam, fought in the war and returned home a drug addict. He never recuperated from the affects of war. In the year of 2000, he went to his Parents' home and shot himself to death in the family room. This young man committed suicide. He found himself unable to handle the residual pressure from the war, and what was expected of him when he returned. Everyone expected him to be strong like his Dad, the Pastor. Peradventure he had some personal trepidation that was never dealt with. We don't know. Perhaps he needed urgent supportive assistance with compassionate care.

The people around him, who loved him most, namely his family, may not have been aware how close he was to giving up. The help he possibly needed may not have reached him in a timely fashion. Bottom line: He saw suicide as his only option to ease the pain. The hurting caused him to check out of this world. Possibly, life's pressures were too much for him to handle. How agonizing it may have been for this son and the family he left behind. We do not care to imagine finding a loved one's body who has committed suicide. Let's pray that by the Grace of God, we never will. I am sure it was a difficult pill to swallow for this precious family. The tragedy must have been devastating, not only for a family of The Reverend Clergy, but for any family experiencing such a lost.

Another Story

The Reverend Oral Roberts and his wife, Evelyn, [*Bless their Memory*] were on Pastor Benny Hinn's program, many years ago. He and his wife gave a testimony about one of their sons taking his life. He couldn't handle the memory of Vietnam and the way the Soldiers were treated upon their return to the United States. People are hurting today, especially those *Living in Glass Houses*. The pain can be excruciating and many times unbearable.

Occasionally, Children, as well relatives of The Reverend Clergy, walk away from Family Ministries. They want nothing to do with the LORD; the Church or anything religious. Some may have left other Family Businesses and/or traditional lifestyles behind. Yet, in ministry, somehow it is felt that the pressures of life akin to religion seen too much to endure. Some of the people, you see sleeping on the streets are not homeless. Many of them, just put a few things in a shopping bag, walked out the door and said good-bye to life as they knew it. They would rather drop out from the religious or social order of community. In frustration, they leave behind the Church, the LORD, and the Family Business – Ministry. I can hear the wheels turning in your heads, asking why? Why would someone do such a thing? Why would they walk away from Family, Friends, Church, Temple, Synagogue, and/or God? Leaving your support group is unheard of. Why walk away from all you have into a life that is often hopeless and unknown?

Who can influence you to do such a thing? Let me tell you who. It is the enemy of your soul, the devil. He is influencing you to do such distressful things to yourself. That is why people tend to hurt those they love and those who love them. Who is your enemy? Your enemy is the adversary – satan. Many people are miserable and unhappy. They want others to be miserable as well. John 10:10 illustrates, three devices the enemy makes use of in dealing with humanity. Jesus said: *"The thief cometh not, but for to steal, and to kill, and to destroy: I am come that they might have life, and that they might have it more abundantly."* I am so glad that Jesus came, that we might have an overflowing Christlike life in Him. The *good news* is that, we can have it more abundantly. Hallelujah!

How Do You See Yourself?

Chapter 3

How do you see yourself? What is the image you see in the mirror? Will you be made whole? Do you have the mental desire to be made whole? Can you see yourself whole? Complete? Review with me the story of Jesus healing an impotent man, on the Sabbath at the feast of the Jews. That certain man had an infirmity for thirty-eight years. He sat beside the pool of Bethesda waiting for the moving of the water. After more than three decades, Jesus came by, and inquired of him: *"Wilt thou be made whole?"* His response was: *"Sir, I have no man."*

Instantly, the man began giving Jesus excuses why he was still in that state after so many years. Someone must have fed him. Somebody had to bathe him and help him with clothing. It stands to reason that others were helping take care of his basic human needs. When you examine his situation, he had to have some assistance. Yet, he gave Jesus an excuse when asked the question: *"Wilt thou be made whole?" "Sir, I have no man."* What do you think about this miraculous event? (Study John 5:1-15)

Are you making excuses for not moving forward? What excuses are you using for sitting on the stool of do nothing, whistling to the tune of do less? What excuses are you giving yourself for not going forward with God, and the things of God? What excuses are you using for leaving the Family Business – Ministry? Do you have doubt going on? Do some self-inventory. First: "To thine own self be true." What do you desire of the Lord? God desires of us a testimony. So simply let go and let God be Glorified in your life. His Grace is sufficient for you, for me and for the entire world. Amen. Amen.

Let's Talk

Our Cleric Parents were chosen, and called by God, to Preach, the *Good News* of the Gospel of Jesus Christ to a lost and dying world. We did not think they were always there for us, but they were. It appeared as if the people at Church and in the community had and still have our Parents more than us. The question on the floor is: Why do you think that is true? I can hear your responses. Someone was always in our home and/or on our telephone, taking our Parents' time away from us. When our family would have an outing, people would come up to our Parents and monopolize their time. This would take their minds off of the event and our family. We came to resent the Ministry, the business, their career and the people ruining our family outings. Do you think this was communicated to our Parents? Most times, it was not. Telling our Parents was not an option. We did not want our Parents to feel badly. After all, they were doing the Lords' work, or working to take care of the family. Does that sound right?

Some of us did not discuss our displeasure with our siblings either. These feelings were oft times suppressed. Our feeling that God would be displeased with us was ever present. There was a fear that God would zap us if we voiced our displeasure with our Parents. Some of us questioned why God chose our Parent(s) to work in His Ministry? Why didn't He choose our neighbors, and/or anyone else, except our Parents? Why were our Parents always in the limelight? Why weren't they just white or blue-collar workers? They didn't have to own the place. The enemy of our souls is constantly talking in our ears, trying to put negative thoughts in our minds. That negativity is rehearsed over and over again. As we rehearse it, negativity gets down into our hearts and spirits. The evil one is constantly throwing accusations in our minds toward our Parents. They are often accused of not loving us and/or being available for us.

Proverbs 6:31: *"But if he be found, he shall restore sevenfold; he shall give all the substance of his house."*

The adversary tries to convince you that your situation would be different if only your Parents were not Preachers. Perhaps you would have received more love and care. They would have more time for you. You could have done this, that or the other, together. People try to convince us that we are not important to our Parents. Others are more important. If Dad and Mom really cared about us, they would try to stay home more with us. They would not accept all those interviews, radio time and/or ministerial engagements. They would tell the 'do-drop-inners' to go home; this is not a good time to visit. You must leave now. The next time, unless it is an emergency, please call before you come.

Was this your life? Is this your life now? Did your Parents continuously leave you alone or with a Sitter? Are you constantly on the road with them and not getting enough rest? Is your answer a resounding YESSSSSSSSSSSSSSS? A thousand times YES. That is and was my life. But, you see, we thought it would have been sacrilegious if they didn't allow people to intrude upon their rights and privacy. Are those your thought processes? Is it a requirement from God to always be available for the masses? It is the right thing to do, right? The calling and gifts your Parents have came from God. Didn't they? They are using their gifts and talents to provide for us, and to help others. Right?

We question why they are allowing this intrusion of our privacy? Why can't we live a normal life like everyone else? Dad was brilliant and very charismatic. He could have chosen another profession. Why didn't he become a Doctor, Lawyer, Teacher or Indian Chief? He didn't have to become a Preacher, a Rabbi, an Actor or a Politician. Mom was also brilliant. Why didn't she pursue greatness in other areas of her life? Why did she feel the need to Preach, instead of act, sing, teach and/or go into commerce? Simply because my Family is from the Tribe of Levi, did that mean my Parents had to become members of the Rabbinic Priesthood? Does that denote that I am called to carry out those same duties? I love God and the things of God, yet I prefer to be in the background, not out front all the time. I am always on display. What's up with that? Children of 'those who serve' enjoy very little private time with their Parents. Frequently, others tend to infringe upon our Family times together. Although God gave us 'Servant Parents'; He also wants us to be happy. I know God loves us. Albeit, the questions on the floor are: "How much longer? When will this all end? Can I please have some 'me' time?" These are a few unspoken questions. Perhaps, you are too fearful of God to voice them out loud.

Let me explain something to you. God is Omnipotent – all-powerful, possessing completeness, unlimited. He is universal in power and authority. God is Omniscient, all-knowing. He is Omnipresent . . . continuously and simultaneously present throughout the whole of creation, everywhere present at the same time. God sees all, hears all, knows all and is in all. There is nothing hidden from Him. We would be petrified if we focused on these facts about God. Yet, it is all about us. We are so focused on the things that we feel we should have, but do not. Facts about the character of God never enter our minds. It is all about us. Know this: God loves you so much that He sent Jesus to die that you might live the abundant life.

Another thing: Stop comparing yourself with Joe Smo, Suzie Q and Lucie Lou. It is wrong for us to compare ourselves with others. II Corinthians 10:12 tells us plainly: *"For we dare not make ourselves of the number, or compare ourselves with some that commend themselves: but they measuring themselves by themselves, and comparing themselves among themselves, are not wise."* Verse 18 advises: *"For not he that commendeth himself is approved, but whom the Lord commendeth."*

Are you comparing your family with others? Do you think their family structure is better than yours? They seen to be so happy. Right? Reality check. The 80/20 rule. Leaving/longing for the 20, when you have the 80 in your hand. Why leave the 80 for the 20? The grass always looks greener on the other side until you get there. You will find that the grass is dead. The perfect family unit on the outside has some dysfunction inside. Your home environment may not be perfect according to you, but neither is theirs. Everyone has some growing to do. In every home, there is disagreement if people live in them. No home is perfect, although we strive for perfection. Enough is enough. O' God, please get me out of this *Glass House* is a constant plea.

The Worst Kind of What?

Chapter 4

Hey, let's have some dialogue? It is time to talk. We need an understanding. Are you there? Children of The Reverend Clergy have the same needs and desires as other Children. *Right?* We desire to be loved and cared for by others. Do you follow? We are Children, born as you were born, who also desire the finer things of life. Still the same with us! We have goals, dreams, and visions. Let us be. Set us free to be men and women, boys and girls. Set us free. Let us enjoy life. Stop trying to take our wings away from us. When you see us attempting to fly, will you help us? Stop with the constant put down and discouragement. Your derogatory words and frowns cut us deep. It sometimes cut to the very core of our being. How many of you have been accused of being *the worst kind?*

The statement, *"Preachers' Kids Are The Worst Kind,"* can hurt you to your heart. It causes one to query the idea. *"We are the worst kind of what?"* What made us *the worst*? Why would God make us *the worst kind*? Out of all of the people in the world, we were picked to be *the worst kind* in the entire world. Why? This question is plaguing Children of The Reverend Clergy until this day. *"We are the worst kind of what?"* Why would such a harmful, negative label be put on Children due to the vocation of their Parents? We would like this statement explained to us.

That statement was first made to me, by a high school teacher. I raised my hand to be excused. Permission was refused. I knew the consequences if I didn't leave the room. My response was: "All due respect, I must be excused." As I left the classroom, the response was clear: *"I always knew that Preachers' Kids are the worst kind."*

Those words rang in my ears as I left the class. Some of the students laughed at the statement. I felt bad. My mind went over that statement. I pondered over and over again, *the worst kind of what*? What were they talking about – *the worst kind?* I only asked to be excused in a respectful manner. *"The worst kind of what?"* I will never forget that class.

As my day progressed, I had to change classes. During an afternoon class, I asked to be excused for the same reason. Again, my request was denied. My response was the same. "With all due respect, I must be excused." As I arose from my desk to leave the room, I heard the same words I had heard earlier echoing in my ears: *"I always knew that Preachers' Kids are the worst kind?" Worst kind of what?* What are we doing as Preachers' Kids that make us so bad? What and/or who are we being compared? In the ladies room while washing my hands, I thought about this statement. Twice in one day, I am being ridiculed by an authority figure, someone I am supposed to look up to in life. What do they see in me? What do they see in us that would cause them to make such a statement? Are we involved in something outrageous? Why are we ostracized in our own communities, cities, states and the world? I looked at myself in the mirror trying to see what they saw. I wanted to know what they saw in me, and others like me, that made us *the worst kind.* I thought I was a Southern Belle. I was an honor roll student. I didn't smoke, drink, gamble, kill, steal, lie, nor flirt around. I tried to be a model Citizen. Although, I spoke my mind; I am not immoral. I said what I thought pretty much. Did that make me *the worst kind?*

When I went home from school that day, my Mom was there, waiting for her Children, with a delicious homemade before dinner snack. I told her about my traumatic experiences in two of my classes. Mom listened very attentively to me. She assured me this matter would be dealt with immediately. My Dad arrived home from work and dinner was served shortly, thereafter. Later in the evening, we had our usual family time. Dad, Mom and some of the Kids sat in chairs while others sat on the floor.

Dad re-iterated to us, that we should never let anyone put us down because of who we are, what we do, or what we do not have, nor because of the color of our skin, size or whatever. We are as good as, and/or better than anyone walking on two feet. In fact, "We are Preachers' Kids." Dad asked about our day. I told Dad what happened at school. My Dad, a very wise man, a loving protective husband, and father asked me how I felt about what was said to me.

I explained to my Dad the impact that statement had on me. After analyzing the statement, my question to Dad was, *"We are the worst kind of what?"* I do not understand why this is said to us and about us. During our early years, my siblings had similar experiences. "Oh how I miss my Dad and Mom." They have both transitioned into their new home in Heaven. *May God Bless Their Memory.*

Dad's explanation helped us to see things from a different perspective. Picture this: It was the segregated South. Professionals in the then Negro [African American] community did not receive the same respect as The Reverend Clergy received from other races, including their own race. The Reverend Clergy received much more respect than the teachers, doctors, lawyers and other professionals in the African American community. As a result of The Reverend Clergy in our community receiving more respect than many who had graduated college; resentment was perceived among the ranks. The Reverend Clergy in our community, and their Offspring were now and then, looked upon with disdain, until there was a need for their services. Maybe, just maybe, this is the source of that erroneous statement: *"Preachers' Kids Are The Worst Kind."* Again the question on the floor is: *"Worst kind of what?"*

The next day, my Mom went to the school and spoke with the principal as well as all of my Teachers, especially the two who made the derogatory statement the day before. After Mom's visit, I never heard that statement from any other authority figure. Dad and Mom assured me the day it happened that the situation would be dealt with immediately and it was. My Dad encouraged his Children to be direct and tell the truth. I tried to obey him with everything that was in me. I was straight to the point. We could not talk back or sass anyone. Hence, sassing our Elders was not and is not an option. It was seen as disrespect. Yet, we are considered the worst kind. *The worst kind of what?* All of us didn't curse, swear and act a fool. We did not steal nor kill. Yet, we are always on display as being *the worst kind.* *"We are Living in Glass Houses."* No matter what we do, or what we say, from time to time, we are ridiculed, insulted and disrespected.

There were Children in our town who were having abortions, flirting around, drinking like fish, committing adultery with married men and/or women, stealing, spending time in jail, smoking, drinking and carousing.

Yet, [we] the Preachers' Kids are considered *the worst kind*. *"The worst kind of what?"* It is repeatedly said, we, the Preachers' Kids are *the worst kind*. *"The worst kind of what?"* We are always on display. People are expecting the worst of us. When they are questioned regarding our behavior, the response is didn't you know that *"Preachers' Kids Are The Worst Kind?"* What is the criterion that they are using? We are under close scrutiny at all times. No matter what we do and or say, we are criticized. If we bought into that negativity, one would believe that they cannot do anything right. But we know that is not true. We are God-fearing, loving, smart, honest individuals who happen to live in *Glass Houses*. Know in your *Knower* that you are fearfully and wonderfully made in the image and likeness of God, Our Heavenly Father.

When we take our rightful place becoming an integral part of the Ministry with our Parents, we are often ostracized and ridiculed. Many have been heard saying: Who do they think they are? Every time I turn around, they are up doing this, that and the other. They are working on my nerves, always on display. They are parading in and out of the Church, on and off the scene. They are taking up the offerings, ushering, and singing on the choir, entertaining us. I am tired of them. They sit their children at the organ and piano and let them bang. They are not that talented. They can play. Why them and not my Children? They think their Children are better than anyone else. Every chance I get I let them know, that they are not all that. My little Jimmie is not given a chance and I am not going to take it anymore. Enough is enough*!!*

When, we, the Children of Those Who Serve, do not participate in the Church and its activities, we are often called *the worst kind*. When we sit quietly in the pews, we are called *the worst kind*. When we are mischievous, we are *the worst kind*. When we participate in all of the Church activities, we are *the worst kind*. No matter what we do, it is not good enough. Will you help me? Help us? We need clarity. We, Preachers' Kids, need an understanding. Why do you all hate us so much? Why do you all dislike us so much? Why are accusatory fingers being pointed in our direction? We will never do anything to hurt you deliberately. We are hurting because of the way you treat us. What is the problem? We, the Preachers' Kids are considered *the worst kind*. My question still is: *"We are the worst kind of what?"*

What will it take for you to accept us as human beings? We bleed the same red blood; breathe the same air. Let us blossom into the men and women, boys and girls God wants us to be. God has a plan and purpose for us; we desire to live in accordant. Will you help us? Your little Johnny gets into trouble. You say they are *worst* than you. They do things *worsted* than this. Again, what are you referring to? Where did the statement *"Preachers' Kids are the worst kind"* originate? If we are to be considered *the worst kind;* what's the source?

I asked that question of one of my friends. This is the answer I received. So much is expected from you all as Preachers' Kids because of who your Parents are. The fact, you were raised by The Reverend Clergy, suggests that you should have more than average morals and values. High standards must always be demonstrated in every facet of our lives. Moral expectations are high. Given this is not the case, our Parents should be held more accountable. They ought to keep a better watchful eye on us. Reverend Clergy Parents should be more loving and accessible to their children. Nevertheless, they must remain welcoming and reachable to their Parishioners. Again, the question on the floor is *"We are the worst kind of what?"*

PKs, just because we are labeled as *the worst kind*, it doesn't make it so, nor makes it true. Say what God says about you.

"AS FAR AS THE EAST IS FROM

THE WEST, SO FAR HATH

HE REMOVED OUR

TRANSGRESSIONS FROM US."

Psalm 99:12

Forgive The Offenders

Chapter 5

Pssst. Pssst. Pssst. I am calling *"The Children of Those Who Serve."* Their service may be in Ministry, Politics, Entertainment, Sport, or any other spotlight. I refer to these Children and family members as *"Those Who Live in Glass Houses."* Bishops, Pastors, Rabbis, Priests, together with all Clerics. This call is for you. I know you have been hurt. Yet, this hurt has been going on for quite some time. It has reached the core of your being. Forgive the antagonist. Forgive those who have hurt you. Forgive those who are hurting you now. Get over it. Forgive the Church members who have made digs at you and your family for generations. Forgive all of the negativity that is aimed at you. The time is now to forgive those who have hurt you. They have gone on with their lives and you are still holding on to their garbage. It is eating you alive from the inside out, and the outside in. Take your life back. One of my Aunts always said: *"Give me back my business so I can go on my way."* Take your life back and give it to God for His service. Amen.

Jesus told us that if we do not forgive, neither will our Heavenly Father forgive us our trespasses. Forgive. Ask God to forgive those individuals who hurt you and help the hurts to stop hurting. We must forgive. Many would trade places with you today if they could. Remember, people only make digs at someone they want to be like. Someone wants to emulate you. See the big picture. People will come at you from all angles, but do not let them discourage you. God is on your side. You can make it.

In Luke 11:1b: *"[O]ne of His disciples said unto Him, Lord, teach us to pray, as John also taught his disciples."* Jesus instructed them how to pray. Verse four [4] says: *"And forgive us our sins; for we also forgive every one that is indebted to us. And lead us not into temptation; but deliver us from evil."*

Example

I was told a story about two men in an office. One was a young man who was about to graduate from college. The other was an elderly man. He was encouraging the graduate to do all and be all he could do and be. He took the younger man to the window. As they looked out, the elderly gentleman asked this question, *"What do you see?"* The response was: *"I see two trees."* Looking a little closer at the trees, he said: *"I see a pecan tree, and a chinaberry tree. Is there anything different about the tree, other than the fruit? Yes. In the pecan tree, there are all kinds of debris, but in the chinaberry tree, there is nothing but chinaberries."* The young man asked why? The elderly man responded this way. *"People only throw at what they are interested in, something they want."*

Children of Those Who Serve, when people tend to come at you from every angle: *"Rejoice, and be exceeding glad: for great is your reward in heaven: for so persecuted they the prophets which were before you."* (Matthew 5:12) Do not hold onto slights, insults, bitterness or anger. Holding onto negative emotions can stop or hinder the flow of God's blessings from moving freely in your life.

Offense is a condemnation attack weapon that the adversary uses against the Children of God. Stop becoming off-ended with people. Do not allow their issues with life to become your problems. Getting caught up in other people lifestyles can hinder your spiritual growth and development. Trust in the LORD with all of your heart. When life seem to be throwing everything at you, no matter what the trials or situations, trust in God. He will see you through. Shake off unforgiveness. See God in the midst of it all. See His hand guiding and directing you and yours. God will victoriously bring you through your challenges. Declare: "LORD, I forgive. Help Thou my unforgiveness. LORD, I forgive John. LORD, I forgive Jane Doe. LORD, I forgive. Thank You Lord for Your forgiveness."

Jesus said: *"For if ye forgive men their trespasses, your heavenly Father will also forgive you: But if ye forgive not men their trespasses, neither will your Father forgive your trespasses."*

(Matthew 6:14-15)

"For I know the thoughts that I think toward you, saith the LORD, thoughts of peace, and not of evil, to bring you an expected end."
(Jeremiah 29:11)

God has good thoughts toward you. He wants great things to happen in your life, but you are allowing unforgiveness to stop it from coming to past in your life. Sure, you may have been hurt by people in your community. You may even have been hurt by Church people, including your family. That is life. Hurt is a reality, not an option. Hurting people, hurt people When we are hurting, we go into a defensive mode. We sometimes go underground into a shelter or a cocoon. We simply shut down. We vow never to let anyone get close enough to hurt us ever again. We put our guard up trying to protect ourselves.

Every time someone enters this forbidden territory that you have closed off – they encounter an attitude second to none. You start acting ugly toward them. It is a sad situation. When you think about the person(s) who hurt you, your blood runs cold. Another vow is made. Never again will anyone hurt me. If anything, I will do the hurting from now on. You are trying to protect yourself against being hurt. Impossible! The more you try to hide your feelings, the more vulnerable you are. Unforgiveness will cause you to become angry, defensive, fearful and paranoid. Job 3:25 declares: *"For the thing which I greatly feared is come upon me, and that which I was afraid of is come unto me."* You become like a magnet drawing all of the things you do not desire to yourself. Unforgiveness leads to worst things. All of those things are hindrances to the blessings of the LORD in your lives.

What do you fear? Why are you so angry at Susie Q and/or Joe Blow? When you see Susie Q and/or Joe Blow your blood runs cold. Why? Think about it. They are not affected by your presence at all, but you are affected by theirs. You are holding a grudge. They have gone on with their lives. If you mentioned to them what you are angry at they would look at you as if you were crazy. You are enslaved by your own unforgiveness. It has you in bondage. Forgive everyone who has hurt you, whether they are alive or dead. Put a chair in front of you. Call the person's name. Say Joe Blow, and/or Susie Q, I forgive you. LORD, I forgive them. Help Thou my unforgiveness. Deliver me from any and everything that will not bring glory and honor to You, LORD.

I choose to love, forgive and forget. I choose total deliverance in every facet of my life. Unforgiveness binds, grips, deters and dominates a person's life. When a person dwells on the negative, look closely and you will see the error. How can you not forgive someone based upon their offense when Jesus has forgiven you for so much? Do not let anyone destroy you. Go to God in prayer and things will change drastically for you.

When the Son makes you free, you shall be free indeed. Does God want you free? Yes, He does. Only God can heal your insides to set you free. Cry out to God today to make you free from the yoke of bondage. Free from torment. Free from anger. Free from everything that has you in bondage. Stand flat-footed on the Word of God. He is the Great Liberator. Depend on Him to make you free.

"And ye shall know the truth, and the truth shall make you free."
(John 8:32)

"If the Son therefore shall make you free, ye shall be free indeed."
(John 8:36)

Let the LORD set you free from the hurts and pains of your past. *"Casting all of your care upon Him; for He careth for you."* (I Peter 5:7) Why are you holding onto the weights of your past? Why have you given that person or those persons so much power over you? You are angry with God, your parents, your selves, situations and so much more. Stop pointing the finger at them and start pointing it at yourselves. You have relinquished your power into the hands of other people. It is time for you to put an end to the blame game. Stop right now. It is eating you alive. Where are you in the scheme of things? What is your part in all of this?

Jesus told us plainly, if we do not forgive, neither will God forgive us. Unforgiveness will cripple you in every area of your life. Harboring unforgiveness in your heart house is not of God. Realize this is a spiritual battle. The enemy of your soul will build a nest in your mind of unforgiveness. As you meditate on it, the unforgiveness seeps into your heart and goes deep down into your spirit. That thing that has offended you is now controlling you on every hand. What must you do to forgive? Did you say forgive? Yes. Forgive so that God will forgive your trespasses. When Jesus was asked by Peter this question, "How many times should I forgive – seven times? Jesus replied in this manner. No, you should not forgive just seven times, but seventy times seven and all in the same day. The bottom line is to forgive.

Forgive!!! Forgive!!! Forgive!!! Oh, one more thing, forgive! Forgive the offender. Forgive the offense. They do not remember what they did or said. If they do remember what they did to you was wrong and do not apologize for the wrong, so what? Get over it. Do not allow other people's issues to become your issues. Why are you holding onto it? It is eating you up like a sickness. It is crippling you. The offender has gone on with their lives. You might say I will forgive but I will not forget. When you rehearse the wrong done to you over and over again, you are giving place to the devil. Jesus told us in the Gospels: If we do not forgive men their trespasses, neither will our Father in heaven forgive us. Forgive. You will feel so much better when you do.

The Bible also encourages us that we should pray without ceasing. Pray for those who have hurt you. Pray for those who have rule over you. Pray for your family and friends. Pray for your country. Pray for the world. Get a prayer partner to agree with you and stand on the promises of God for your situation. Getting some-one to agree with you is one of the hardest things to do. If you can find an Agree-er, apply this scripture when the two of you agree. Jesus said: *"Verily I say unto you, Whatsoever ye shall bind on earth shall be bound in heaven: and whatsoever ye shall loose on earth shall be loosed in heaven. Again I say unto you, That if two of you shall agree on earth as touching any thing that they shall ask, it shall be done for them of my Father which is in heaven. For where two or three are gathered together in My name, there am I in the midst of them."* (Matthew 18:18-20)

What does it mean to take this most seriously? Jesus is saying that we should consider all He has said to the greatest extent. Take what He said to heart. Use it as we pray together. Remember what the Bible is saying to us. Touch and agree with your prayer partner. Let's look again at Matthew 18:19, and process what it is saying to us. Jesus said: *"Again*

I say unto you, That if two of you shall agree on earth as touching any thing that they shall ask, it shall be done for them of My Father which is in heaven." Find someone to agree with you via the telephone, in person, over the internet and/or through the mail. Find an Agree-er, and put God in remembrance of His Word. Stand on His promises, and watch them come to past in your lives. After you are delivered from the snare of the enemy; by faith, walk into your blessings that God has prepared for you. "But as it is written, EYE HATH NOT SEEN, NOR EAR HEARD, NEITHER HAVE ENTERED INTO THE HEART OF MAN, THE THINGS WHICH GOD HATH PREPARED FOR THEM THAT LOVE HIM." (I Corinthians 2:9)

"To Every Thing There Is A Season"

Chapter 6

"This is the day which the LORD hath made; we will rejoice and be glad in it." (Psalm 118:24)

This is your season; walk into it. God made this day for us, all of us. What are we going to do with it? We have been given so much but we are not using it. It is time. It is your time. Walk into your season of blessings, miracles, health, Ministry and all of the things God has given to you. What an honor and a privilege to be called a son and/or daughter of God. What an honor and a privilege to spread the Good News of Jesus Christ. It is indeed an honor and a privilege to live the abundant life in Christ on a daily basis. It is an honor and a privilege to be Children of The Reverend Clergy.

Just think . . . God chose you to be a part of the lineage to proclaim the message regarding His dear Son. He sees your heart, and knows that He can use you and your family to bring souls into a saving knowledge of Jesus Christ. The ability to carry the weight of the anointing in and of itself is an awesome responsibility. It is also a humbling realization that God would trust someone like you with His creation. My *late* brother, David, when negativity came his way, would say: "Shake it right off." We must shake off the old unregenerate man with his deeds, and be renewed by the Spirit of God. Ask God to give you clear direction, and allow Him to order your steps. Psalm 119:133-134 prays: *"Order my steps in Thy word: and let not any iniquity have dominion over me. Deliver me from the oppression of man: so will I keep Thy precepts."*

God wants to order your steps. You must let Him. Give Him permission to guide and direct the affairs of your life. Jesus promised never to leave you nor forsake you. God's promises are sure and Amen. What is promised in the Word of God is real. Make the Word real in your lives by applying it on a daily basis. Don't become obsessed with material things. Be content with what you have. Hebrews 13:5-6 exhorts us: *"Let your conversation be without covetousness; and be content with such things as ye have: for He hath said, I WILL NEVER LEAVE THEE, NOR FORSAKE THEE. So that we may boldly say, THE LORD IS MY HELPER, AND I WILL NOT FEAR WHAT MAN SHALL DO UNTO ME."*

Trust in God and stop feeling sorry for yourself. Cease the endless mind chatter. Allow God to order your steps. Psalm 37:23 declares: *"The steps of a good man are ordered by the LORD: and He delighteth in his way."* Accept the fact that God ordained your Parents and Family for Ministry. You cannot change that fact. You cannot change your DNA. You were not born into your family by mistake. It was by God's design. It is not a mistake that your [our] Parents are members of The Reverend Clergy. Some are: Bishops, Pastors, Preachers, Rabbis, Priests, Evangelists, Missionaries, Deacons, etc. No, it is not a mistake that our Parents are labors, 'together with God' of those who serve. You were chosen as constituents of the Family of God. We are who we are by Divine appointment. It is important for us to learn to love, and accept who we are. We were fearfully and wonderfully made in the image and likeness of God our Father. The blessings of your Parent(s), and my Parents are being passed on from generation to generation. Amen.

Do not resent God, or the things of God. He loves you. He did not cause the pain and heartache you may experience from time to time. Hurting and pain come from the enemy of your soul. God want what is best for you and yours. He loves you with an everlasting love. He has drawn you with loving kindness unto Himself. Satan, the enemy of your soul use people to orchestrate situations and circumstances causing you to doubt the love of God. Do not allow the adversary to do such a thing. I encourage you to forget the past and begin to dream again. Dare to dream and dream big dreams. See yourself in your dream. Have a vision of your desired end. Remember: "Without a vision the people perish." So set goals: long term, and short term. Relentlessly pursue them. Go after them with a passion. Do not let anyone or anything deter you from reaching your desired end. Throw caution to the wind. It is time to get out of the boat. Walk on water and go to Jesus. You have been hurting for years, but this is your time. This is your season to soar like an eagle. I am reminded of a scripture that says:

"But they that wait upon the LORD shall renew their strength; they shall mount up with wings as eagles; they shall run, and not be weary; and they shall walk, and not faint."

(Isaiah 40:31)

You have been hindered for so long. The enemy has waged war on you. Didn't you know Jesus conquered death, hell and the grave? He gave all power into our hands. Satan is a defeated foe. I have a question to ask you. Do you know? Are you aware? In Jesus Christ, we won! Amen. Hallelujah! The battle is not your battle, but the battle belongs to the LORD. I looked in the back of the Bible – we have already won. When Jesus died on Calvary, He said: "IT IS FINISHED." The work that He was sent to do has been completed.

Prodigal son, or daughter, you have wasted all of your inheritance. All of your money is gone. You would have eaten corncobs in the slop trough but no one would give them to you. Shake yourself off. As you do, the blinders will come off your eyes and you will see that your father has more than enough for you. You will see how much your family loves and miss you. Dust yourself off and return home. What will it take for you to get up out of the hog pen? Will you come home? Swallow your pride and come home. No one is waiting to point a finger at you. They are waiting to love you past your dysfunction. They desire to love you in spite of your obvious hurts and pain. Take the sting out of it. Tell your loved ones that you thought you were right, but you were wrong. Ask them to forgive you for all you have done to hurt the family. Tell them you want to come home. You have come to yourself. Do not try to justify your wrong way of thinking any longer. It is not necessary. Get up now and go home.

Get up I said. Come out of the pigpen. Come out of it now. Stop eating the slop that was put in the hog trough. You have been in that hog pen far too long. You have wallowed in the mud far too long. Come home. Your family is waiting for you. While there is breath in your body, come home. Prodigal son and/or daughter: "It is time for you to come home where you belong." Get out of the mud. Come home where you belong. You have been sorely missed. Your family needs you to come home. They want you to come home. They love you. They realize you are hurting. They can feel your pain. Let them help you get through this pain. It is your restoration season. Repent. Simply make a 180-degree turn-around. Receive your total restoration in all things. It is yours. It is time to receive all that God has for you. God has liberated and set you free from the yoke of bondage. Stay free. John 8:36 reminds us that: *"If the Son therefore shall make you free, ye shall be free indeed."*

"Stand fast therefore in the liberty wherewith Christ hath made us free, and be not entangled again with the yoke of bondage."
(Galatians 5:1)

Walk, live, move, breathe and bask in the liberty that has made you free. It is yours to savor and enjoy. Stop making apologies for being born to Parents or a Parent in Ministry. Stop making apologies for who you are and your inheritance. The devil has got to loosen your belongings. Change your posture and position. You shall surely recover it all. Don't you know that you are destined for greatness? There is nothing that you put your mind to do that you cannot accomplish. God has some wonderful things in store for you. Be proud that your Parents are working in the vineyard of Almighty God, the Creator of this Universe. Your rewards, in the Kingdom of God can surpass any investment in a Success 1000 company in the world.

"And David enquired at the LORD, saying, Shall I pursue after this troop? shall I overtake them? And he answered him, Pursue: for thou shalt surely overtake them, and without fail recover all."
(I Samuel 30:8)

Put your eyes on Jesus and keep them there. Be strong in the Lord and in the power of His might. Put on the whole armor of God that you might be able to stand against the wiles of the devil in the evil day. Take courage. Stop the whining. Quit whimpering. Don't be a jelly-back. Make the decision to change your posture and position. Rebuke indecision. Denounce all negativity. Stop the endless mind chatter. Do not allow the adversary to control your mind. Today, there is an unusual battle going on for the minds of men, especially in this new digital era. Yet, you have the victory in Christ Jesus. This, too, is a victorious season. However, it is imperative that you search out and find the will of God for your life. Get your thinking aligned with the Word of God. Straighten your life out. Don't confer with flesh and blood regarding it anymore. Seek God with all of your heart. Remember, the LORD Prayer. Jesus said to His Disciples: *"When ye pray, say, Our Father which art in heaven, Hallowed be Thy name. Thy kingdom come. Thy will be done, as in heaven, so in earth. Give us day by day our daily bread."* (See Luke 11:1-4) This is God's abundance prayer. Heaven on earth is God's perfect will. So get your plan and purpose in life complete. Life is a journey, not a sprint. Micah presents this question to us all.

"He hath shewed thee, O man, what is good; and what doth the LORD require of thee, but, to do justly, and to love mercy, and to walk humbly with thy God?" (Micah 6:8)

Are you fulfilling God's requirement of you? God has shown you and told you in His Word what His requirements are. What are you doing with them? He wants you to be men and women of integrity in and out of the home. Humble yourselves in the natural and spiritual. This is a requirement from God. Jesus came meek and lowly, humble and Holy. It is very important to be merciful. *"Blessed are the merciful for they shall obtain mercy."* Humility can take you to higher heights and deeper depths than you have ever known. Humbling yourselves before God means that you realize you were created to serve Him. You are also serving God while serving those around you. If you are a Minister, your first responsibility is to serve others. God has opened many doors for you. Walk through the open doors. This is your season. Walk into it.

See yourself prosperous. See yourself in leadership positions. See yourselves as Chief Executive Officers (CEOs) and Chief Executive Officers (CFOs) of Success 1000 companies. See yourselves the head and not the tail in every situation. "To every thing there is a season." Philippians 4:6 says: *"Be careful for nothing; but in every thing by prayer and supplication with thanksgiving let your requests be made known unto God."* Realizing these words of advice, should encourage us all to travel within the seasons of the positive seeds we have sown. I encourage you to be proactive; do not wait for something to happen. By the Grace of God, determine to let Him make good things happen in your life. Seek after God for what you want with all diligence. Find your niche [God's will] in your life and pursue it. Never allow anyone to stop you from reaching your desired end. Matthew 19:26b reminds us: *"With men this is impossible; but with God all things are possible."* Amen.

Rev. Dr. Arnetha Bowens

To Every Thing There Is A Season . . .

"To every thing there is a season,
      and a time to every purpose
            under the heaven:
A time to be born, and a time to die;
      a time to plant, and a time to pluck up
            that which is planted;
A time to kill, and a time to heal;
A time to break down, and a time build up;
A time to weep, and a time to laugh;
A time to morn, and a time to dance;
A time to cast away stones, and a time to gather stones together;
A time to embrace, and a time to refrain from embracing;
A time to get, and a time to lose;
      a time to keep, and a time to cast away;
A time to rend, and a time to sew;
      a time to keep silence, and a time to speak;
A time to love, and a time to hate;
      a time of war, and a time of peace."
(Ecclesiastes 3:1-8)

Be Aware of Hindrances

Chapter 7

The book of Nehemiah tells us a story of the Jews in Babylonian exile. Nehemiah was concerned for the welfare of Jerusalem and the inhabitants thereof. He desired to rebuild the walls of Jerusalem which was his homeland. It was in ruins. He wanted to protect the individuals that were still dwelling there.

The name Nehemiah in the Hebrew means "Comfort of Yahweh." He heard about the state of affairs of his people; the affliction, distress and reproach. The Walls of Jerusalem were broken down, and the gates were burned. He explained these severe hardships in the book's early chapters. Thus, Nehemiah intercedes with God. He puts a petition before King Artaxerxes and was granted permission to assess the situation in Jerusalem. When he arrived at Jerusalem, the broken walls of the city were inspected. Nehemiah exhorted the people to be resolute. Yet, he had his work cut out for him. He kept records of the builders, and recorded everything he did. Albeit, when his enemies came up against him, he answered them. He was met with much opposition through threats of discouragement, attack, extortion, compromise, slander, treachery, and was openly ridiculed. However, it did not stop him from completing the vision and task that he was given – reconstructing the Wall of Jerusalem. (See Nehemiah 1:1-11.)

Let's focus our attention on Chapter 6 verses 1-4. Nehemiah and his helpers were rebuilding the walls of Jerusalem. They were minding their own business. Although they were busy rebuilding the wall, their enemies were also busy trying to hinder the completion of this great project. When the wall had been complete but not the gates, Nehemiah received a false message requesting his presence in a bogus meeting. He declined the request. Verse 3 gives the response Nehemiah sent to his enemies. "I am doing a great work, so that I cannot come down; why should the work of the Lord cease, while I leave it, and come down to you?" Wouldn't you know that they were persistent in Verse 4 and sent unto him four additional times? His response was always the same.

There is nothing new under the sun. Rest assuredly; henchmen have been dispatched to hinder the Work that God has called you to do. They will use everything at their disposal to stop you in your tracks. He doesn't always show up looking, sounding and acting like the devil and his crowd. He comes as an angel of light. He will also use whomsoever he can to stop you. He will use those persons closest to you if they allow him to use them. The vessel he is operating in is not always an enemy. Sometimes it is a family member, friend and/or associate.

When your enemies come up against you to hinder your progress, what are you answering them? Are you leaving the call of God on your lives to answer your critics? Are you allowing your enemies to rule over you? Remember, Ephesians 6:12 affirms that you are *not wrestling against flesh and blood,* but against principalities and powers. The individuals are not your enemies. Your enemy is the evil spirit using them. What is the motivating force behind that person or situation? Check it out.

The adversary may try to keep the people of God from realizing the love of Christ in their lives. Satan would like to ascend above God by declaring enmity among God's people. God may permit things to play out in our lives. He desires for His people to decree: "Yes, God is Real." Trust Him and cast all your cares on Him; that's the bottom line. The enemy may want to destroy you; however, all you have to do is to let God arise in your life. He will never leave you nor forsake you. God is in control of your life. *"(For the weapons of our warfare are not carnal, but mighty through God to the pulling down of strong holds;)"* (II Corinthians 10:4) You can always trust and rely upon the Word of God. Amen. Hallelujah!

"Lest satan should get an advantage of us: for we are not ignorant of his devices." (II Corinthians 2:11)

We are not ignorant of satan's devices. Jesus reveals three devices in John 10:10. *"The thief cometh not, but for to steal, and to kill, and to destroy: I am come that they might have life, and that they might have it more abundantly."* Live your life to its' fullest; let God's joy overflow *"[F]or the joy of the LORD is your strength.."* (Nehemiah 8:10d) The thief is a destroyer of homes, murderer of babies, causes doubt, fear, unbelief and untold pain. He is also an accuser of the Brethren. You may not aware of it, but the enemy will speak lies in the ears of others about you. They may despise you without a cause. Nonetheless, always know with confidence, that *"We are not ignorant of his [satan's] devices."* Praise God!!!

Some people in your home, church and family are carriers for the evil one. Recognize his deception. His primary aim is to get you out of the will of God. He will try to cause you to run ahead of God. He seeks to hurt God by hurting His creation. Don't get ahead of yourself; satan is a liar and the father of lies. Lies spoken consistently, if not checked, will become truth in the mind. Satan will use lies and falsities to discourage and deceive us. However, Psalm 101:7 reminds us that: *"He that worketh deceit shall not dwell within My house: he that telleth lies shall not tarry in My sight."* Some of these falsities seem believable. That is one of the reasons there is so much deception within Houses of Worship. God said in the Bible that a liar would not tarry in His sight. Lying is listed in Proverbs 6:16-19 as one of the seven things the LORD hates. A lying tongue is the second thing mentioned on the list.

Do not allow liars to empty garbage into your spirit; make nests in your mind and/or heart. It is so important to cast down imaginations and every high thing that tries to exalt itself against the knowledge of God. It is time to pull down the satanic strongholds in your life and your family. Realize this: Jesus defeated satan on the Cross at Calvary more than 2000 years ago. Satan is a defeated foe, not going to be. He is a defeated foe, now. Do not allow him to gain dominion over you and yours. The Bible states this truth to us: *"When the enemy comes up against you one way, the LORD will cause him to flee before you in seven different ways."* Trust God.

Be Watchful

First Peter 5:8 gives the following warning: Be watchful. *"Be sober, be vigilant; because your adversary the devil, as a roaring lion, walketh about, seeking whom he may devour:"* Be aware of your surroundings. Do not walk around with blinders on. Take them off so that you can see. You also must have a clear head in this life. Do not live in a state of intoxication. Be serious and thoughtful in your demeanor and/or quality of life. An understanding of the facts, not speculation, should be your foundation. Know who you are and where you are going. When you know yourself and are secure in God, you can stand the test of time. Resist the devil. How do you resist him? You fight back with the Word of God. In Luke 4:4-10, when Jesus was tempted by the devil; Jesus gave him the Word of God. Take back what the devil has stolen from you through God's Son, Jesus Christ. Stop the mind chatter! You are not wrestling against flesh and blood according to Ephesians 6:12. What does it say? *"For we wrestle not against flesh and blood, but against principalities, against powers, against the rulers of the darkness of this world, against spiritual wickedness in high places."*

Satan is limited in what he can do. He doesn't know everything; God does. He is not everywhere present at the same time, but God is. God is the Creator. Satan is a created being. I encourage you to get to know the Creator for yourself. When satan comes to trouble you, tell God about it. Continue seeking God until He intervenes on your behalf. Matthew 6:33 advises: *"But seek ye first the kingdom of God, and His righteousness; and all these things shall be added unto you."* Satan cannot read your mind. So cast down negative thoughts, recognizing they are not from God. James 4:7 enlightens us, *"Submit yourselves therefore to God. Resist the devil, and he will flee from you."* Scripture says: Submit to God, Resist the devil, he will flee from us. It doesn't say, he might, nor perhaps. When we surrender to God; resist the devil; he *will* flee from us. Amen.

Know who you are in Christ Jesus. Do you really know who you are? Do you believe everything that you hear? Are you gullible? Vulnerable Christians are likely to believe almost anything they are told. They believe most Preachers. They tend to go everywhere to get hands laid on them. Someone told me a story about attending a Tent Meeting. She went down for prayer. The Preacher hit her head so hard, she could barely see. For hours, she wasn't able to drive. Friends took her to their home, nearby. They gave her pain medication and permitted her to rest. She is still "going down for prayer" shy. A beloved Mother, whose son was a Preacher, had an urgent need early one morning. She called several renown Prayer Ministries. Some asked, when she had last given to their work? One Ministry asked her if she were really saved? She called and called to no avail. She could not find anyone willing to agree with her in prayer that morning. Finally, she said, the Holy Spirit revealed to her: "You are calling all over the world looking for prayer, when I have given you your own son". She called her son. Half asleep, he prayed and agreed with his Mom. They are both in heaven now. Yet, it has been more than 25 years and God's answer to her prayer request is still standing firm. God is faithful.

Some are always looking for a word. Sometimes words are spoken from counterfeits such as *God told me to tell you*. Do you know that *these are dangerous words?* Satan comes as an angel of light. God told me. God told me. God told me this, that, or the other. God speaks to us through signs, wonders, people, the Bible, dreams, visions and in an audible voice. Be cognizant of this truth, that our only confirmation is the Word of God. *"God, who at sundry times and in divers manners spake in time past unto the fathers by the Prophets, Hath in these last days spoken unto us by His Son, whom He hath appointed heir of all things, by whom also He made the worlds;"* (Hebrews 1:2-3)

Watch and pray that you do not fall into temptation. Be sure you know who is laboring among you and yours. You should put your faith in Christ. It is time for you to know in whom you believe. The Bible tells us to be persuaded that He [God] is able to keep everything that we have committed into His hands against that day. We are the righteousness of God in Christ Jesus. You must know who you are, and always be watchful and in prayer. *"Watch ye and pray, lest ye enter into temptation. The spirit truly is ready, but the flesh is weak."* (Mark 14:38)

"THE BLESSING OF THE LORD,

IT MAKETH RICH, AND HE ADDETH

NO SORROW WITH IT."

Proverbs 10:22

Discovering Your Enemy

Chapter 8

Who is your enemy? Who has betrayed you? Why did you leave your comfort zone for a wilderness experience? This is a reality check*!* It was not and is not God, who was/is your enemy. Your loving and protective Heavenly Father is not your enemy. Your Clergy Parent(s) or guardian is not your enemy. Satan is the enemy of your soul.

"The thief cometh not, but for to steal, and to kill, and to destroy; I am come that they might have life, and that they might have it more abundantly." (John 10:10)

We are not ignorant of satan's devices. Three devices are illustrated here: They are to *steal* from you, *kill your dreams and desires,* and to ultimately *destroy* you. Jesus said, I am come that you might have and enjoy life to the fullest and until it overflows. Think about it, satan has three obliterating devices. These devices have destroyed thousands, if not millions of individuals, because they didn't use the Word of God. When in a spiritual struggle, or combat with the enemy, use God's Word. The Word of God will tear down satanic strongholds in your life and the lives of your loved ones.

Jesus was led into the wilderness to be tempted of the devil. When tempted, He quoted the Word of God to the devil. Jesus said, *"It is written. It is written. It is written."* When we are tempted and tried, it is essential that we follow our Savior's lead. Tell the enemy of your soul: *"It is written." God said it.* It is so. It will come to to pass. Expect it. What you had was stolen from you and your family by the enemy of your soul. He came to steal your birthright, your influence and your peace. He came to kill you and your influence. The attack is on. The weakest link in your armor is under attack. The object is to kill you and all those looking up to you.

Words Have Power

He wants to destroy you, your family, your reputation and ultimately your life. You are destroyed with the words of your own mouth. What are you saying? Words have creative power. *"For by thy words thou shalt be justified, and by thy words thou shall be condemned."* (Matthew 12:37) You can speak negative things into existence in your life. Your speech needs to change. Your attitude needs to change. You need to renew your mind with the Word of God. Stop saying things like, I almost laughed myself to death. I know this will not work. Stop speaking negative words over your lives. Your mind needs to be changed. You might say, "What do you mean, my mind needs to change?" If a man can control his mouth, he can control his entire body. You need a changed mind.

Romans 12:1-2: *"I beseech you therefore, brethren, by the mercies of God, that ye present your bodies a living sacrifice, holy, acceptable unto God, which is your reasonable service. And be not conformed to this world: but be ye transformed by the renewing of your mind, that ye may prove what is that good, and acceptable, and perfect, will of God."*

He who controls your mind will control your whole body. Who is controlling your mind? The scripture says: *"Let this mind be in you, which was also in Christ Jesus:"* (Philippians 2:5) *"This I say then, Walk in the Spirit, and ye shall not fulfill the lust of the flesh."* (Galatians 5:16) What does that mean? It means you have a choice. Let the mind of Christ be your mind, not some other mind. The choice is yours. Choose now this day who you will serve. Will you serve God or man? Will you allow God or the devil to control your mind, your flesh and your destiny?

"But He giveth more grace. Wherefore he saith, God resisteth the proud, but giveth grace unto the humble." (James 4:6)

"Likewise, ye younger, submit yourselves unto the elder. Yea, all of you be subject one to another, and be clothed with humility: for God resisteth the proud, and giveth grace to the humble."

(I Peter 5:5)

"Love not the world, neither the things that are in the world. If any man love the world, the love of the Father is not in him. For all that is in the world, the lust of the flesh, and the lust of the eyes, and the pride of life, is not of the Father, but is of the world. And the world passeth away, and the lust thereof: but he that doeth the will of God abideth for ever." (I John 2:15-17)

"The fear of the LORD is to hate evil: pride, and arrogancy, and the evil way, and the froward mouth, do I hate." (Proverbs 8:13)

Make A Fresh Start

Find a fresh place to start over again. Make up your mind to change your posture and position. Let go of the bad and sometimes the good. Stop trying to bring your past into your future. Forget those things which are behind. It will not satisfy. You can't relive those years. Yesterday is gone. Stop living with regret. Getting rid of regret means you are making better choices. It comes to a point that it is just you and God. What are you doing with God? It is time to choose life. Stop saying I wish, I would have, should have, could have. Stop now and Live.

We make choices. Every choice we make affects our bloodline. The power of right choices is so amazing. Make the choice. God's arm is not short. He will pick you up out of the muck and miry clay. He will establish your comings and your goings because you are near and dear to Him. You must choose His love and protection. Choose His guidance and direction. Choose to serve the True and Living God. He always provides new beginnings regardless of your situation. He knows what you need, when you aren't aware of your own need.

Jesus said: *"I AM that I AM." I AM here right now. Why are you afraid?* None of your weaknesses matter to God. Let God change your mess into your testimony, your ministry. God chooses the weak things of the world to confound the wise. Stop discounting yourself. Stop looking at your inadequacies. See God. Stop looking at the giants in the land. They have already been defeated. Just realize and know that God is greater than everything and everyone. Stop allowing your past to manipulate your present. Stop letting your present control your future. I dare you to give

God your mess and watch Him make miracles out of it. True repentance leads to sweeping change. You can't tie Jesus into your messes. God has a perfect plan laid out for you in accordance to Ephesians 2:10: *"For we are His workmanship, created in Christ Jesus unto good works, which God hath before ordained that we should walk in them."*

STOP! Stop right there. If you are not living for Jesus, you may be miserable. It is time to get a fresh start. Get your heart in tuned with Jesus. Totally commit to Him. Experience a radical change in your lives, in your situations, family, and every facet of your lives. God has a great life in store for us. We must change our attitudes. Let go and let God. You need a fresh start. If you are resisting God in any area of your life, it will turn out badly for you.

God is the God of second chances, according to Isaiah 43:18-21. *"Remember ye not the former things; neither consider the things of old. Behold, I will do a new thing; now it shall spring forth; shall ye not know it? I will even make a way in the wilderness, and rivers in the desert. The beast of the field shall honour Me, the dragons and the owls: because I give water in the wilderness, and waters in the desert, to give drink to My people, My chosen. This people have I formed for Myself; they shall shew forth My praise."* Forget about what has happened; don't keep going over old history. Be alert, be present. God is about to do something brand new. It's bursting out all around you. Can't you see it? There it is! I'm making a road through the desert, rivers in the badlands for you. Even wild animals seem to say: *Thank You!* – coyotes and buzzards – Because I provided water in the desert, rivers through the sun-baked earth, Drinking water for the people I chose, the people I made especially for Myself, a people custom made to praise Me."

"Therefore if any man be in Christ, he is a new creature: old things are passed away; behold, all things are become new."
(II Corinthians 5:17)

Prayers for Deliverance and Salvation

LORD GOD, in the Name of Jesus, I need You to change my heart. Make me brand-new, today. I desire You to mold, shape and make me according to Your divine will. *"Create in me a clean heart, O God; and renew a right spirit within me. Cast me not away from Thy presence; and take not Thy holy spirit from me. Restore unto me the joy of Thy salvation; and uphold me with Thy free spirit."* (Psalm 51:10-12) [Verses 14 and 15 seeks God's precise rescue.] *"Deliver me from blood guiltiness, O God, Thou God of my salvation: and my tongue shall sing aloud of Thy righteouisness. O Lord, open Thou my lips; and my mouth shall shew forth Thy praise."* O God, I confess my need of total deliverance. Please purge me thoroughly. Sanctify me wholly, spirit, soul, mind and body. Save and deliver me LORD God. Thank you for hearing and answering my prayer. I come to You in this prayer of repentance in the Name of the LORD Jesus Christ. And by faith, it is done. Amen.

GOD, be merciful to me a sinner. I have sinned before God and man. I repent for all the wrong that I have done. I forsake my sin and all worldly offenses. LORD Jesus, come into my heart and become Lord and Master of my life. Live in me, LORD Jesus. Wash me thoroughly from all my sins in Your Precious Blood. Have Your way in my life. Take out my stony heart, and give me a heart of flesh. LORD, I surrender all to You. Thank You, for giving me Your free gift of eternal life. I receive Jesus as LORD of my life. By faith, it is done, in Jesus name. Amen. Amen. Luke 18:13c: *"God be merciful to me a sinner."*

Father God, in the Name of Jesus, Your word said, *"Let us therefore come boldly unto the throne of grace, that we may obtain mercy, and find grace to help in time of need."* (Hebrews 4:16) Father, here I am. I am coming before You, putting You in remembrance of Your word. Isaiah 43:25-26 declares: *"I, even I, am He that blotteth out thy transgressions for Mine own sake, and will not remember thy sins. Put Me in remembrance: let us plead together: declare thou, that thou mayest be justified."* Another verse, Jeremiah 30:17a promises: *"For I will restore health unto thee, and I will heal thee of thy wounds, saith the LORD;"* Matthew 15:26 says: *"But He [Jesus] answered and said, It is not meet to take the children's bread, and to cast it to dogs."* It is seen here that healing is the children's bread. Again, Your word tells us in James 5:15: *"And the prayer of faith shall save the sick, and the Lord shall raise him up; and it he have committed sins, they shall be forgiven him."* Father God in the name of Jesus, we believe Your word. We daily apply Your word to our lives. *"And ye shall serve the*

LORD your God, and he shall bless thy bread, and thy water; and I will take sickness away from the midst of thee." (Exodus 23:25) Hallelujah!

LORD God, Your Son, Jesus Christ, took thirty-nine stripes for my healing. So I claim my healing right now. We are reminded that healing is the children's bread. LORD, I am Your child. You are my healer. Your word makes known that Jehovah-Rapha is my Healer. He is my Doctor in a sick room, my Advocate in all situations. Father, in the name of Jesus, let your healing virtue flow throughout my body; from the crown of my head to the very bottom of my feet. By faith, it is done. Amen. Amen.

Preachers' Kids, Let's Talk

Chapter 9

Hey you. Are you talking to me? Yes, you. Preachers' Kids, also known as PKs. We need to talk. Talk? What do you mean talk? Let's talk now. What are we going to talk about? Let's discuss your life as a PK. We need to talk about challenges to *LIVING IN A GLASS HOUSE; LIVING IN A BUBBLE; AND LIFE UNDER A MICROSCOPE. What is it like* living with *Paparazzi* following you around? Your response is important. Let's talk.

Your Parent(s) may be a Bishop, Minister, Pastor, Evangelist, Missionary, Rabbi, Priest, Prophet, Prophetess, Teacher, Deacon, etc. Their lives are on display, up for public scrutiny, but not yours. The lives of your Parents are open books. You are having issues sharing your Cleric Parent(s) with the public and their involvement. You may wish to share your life experiences with an individual(s) of your choice.

People are watching your every move. You cannot go anyplace and/or do anything without someone watching you and/or eavesdropping on your conversation. You are yelling internally; leave me alone. My life is not an open book. My Dad and Mom's lives were open books. However, not mine. I want to be a normal person. I want to play, laugh, and make merry with my friends. I want to run and jump. I want to play sports. I want to go shopping. I want to dress down. My Parent(s) and/or Guardian(s) are Ministers, not me. Please, leave me alone. Let me live my life. Stop comparing me with and/or to your Children.

You are being compared with the Children of the laity. Non-Preachers' Kids can do whatever they want when they want. They drink, smoke, curse, party and do all kinds of things, but nothing is said. They are watching every step a Preachers' Kids make. We are expected to be perfect because of our Minister Parent(s). If there are flaws in our lives, then their children tend to be off the hook. Non-Preachers' Kids are often told from childhood, if the Preachers' Kids aren't perfect, how can we expect perfection from our children. Preachers Kids live with the Reverend Clergy, yet some of them live such ragged and unholy lives. You are children of the laity; go on with your lives, sow your wild oats. Whatever you can do just do it. It is okay if you act unseemly; but not the Preachers' Kids; they must be examples for others.

As a PK, if you sneeze wrong, it can be held against you. If you laugh out loud, there is an issue. Your clothes have issues. Everything you do is wrong. You are told that you will never measure up to their kids. You will never be anything. *"Preachers' Kids Are The Worst Kind."* It is time to nip this garbage in the bud. People are jealous of you and your family. They want the name recognition you have. God has called your family into Ministry. All Preachers' Kids are called into some kind of Ministry. Some into the pulpit, some into street Ministry, some into the music Ministry, some Social Services, some into fundraising Ministry, some teachers, some prayer warriors, some maintenance, some prison Ministry, some addiction Ministry, some hospitality, some kitchen Ministry, some Missionaries, some Children's Ministry, some administration, some healthcare, some legal, some education, and some are ushers and greeters, etc. Wherever God plants you and whatever is needed is Ministry. Come as you are, and let God make you what He wants you to be.

"For we are labourers together with God: ye are God's husbandry, ye are God's building." (I Corinthians 3:9)

Who are you? Why are you here? How can I expect to go back to who I was before the hurt? You are a Preachers' Kids. You are here as an extension of God's arms to Minister to the needs of mankind. We all have a calling on our lives. We need to find the real role. Who are you really? Why are you here? Find excitement and passion in the process of who you are. My Dad taught us that no one is better than you. You are as good as or better than anyone walking on two feet. Take your life back. Delete all negative messages. Mark them: *"Return to Sender. Addressee Unknown."*

Reject all negative messages regardless of the sender. One part of the whole armor of God is the Shield of Faith where you are able to quench the fiery darts of the wicked. The fiery darts of the wicked are words. The book of James in the Bible talks about the tongue being an unruly member that we use to bless God and curse men. The tongue is full of deadly poisons a world of iniquity. Proverbs says a man is snared by the words of his mouth. Watch what you say. The world was made by God's Words. God created the world with the power of His Words. In the book of Genesis chapter one, the Scripture says that He said, He said, He said several times. Then the scripture said, He saw what He said. We have the same power in our words. Job said, *"Thou shall also decree a thing, and it shall be established unto thee: and the light shall shine upon thy ways."* (Job 22:28)

There is power in words. Matthew 12:37 advises: *"For by thy words thou shalt be justified, and by thy words thou shalt be condemned."* Words matter! *"Death and life are in the power of the tongue: and they that love it shall eat the fruit thereof."* (Proverbs 18:21) Words have creative power, especially, the words spoken after I am. 'I AM' are two of the most powerful words in the English language. You can speak good or bad things into existence using I AM. These two words can shape or break an individual's life. So direct each word before you say or write it behind I AM.

Examples of The Potency of "I AM"

Moses asked God who should I say sent me? God's answer was "I AM that I AM." I AM the Self-Existent One, The Eternal, The One Who Always Has Been And Always Will Be. This is shortened to I AM Here, The Ever-Present and Living One. It is equivalent to GOD, The Eternal.

Cassius Clay, also known as: Mohammed Ali, proclaimed many years ago, *I AM The Greatest*. During his entire boxing career, he remained *The Greatest*. Today, to most Americans, he still is seen as *The Greatest*.

Stop Trying to Please Man

Sometime ago, I heard this story. The truth and the lie were taking a bath. Lie finished first and dried off, putting on the truths clothing. People saw him walking down the street and said, "There is the lie dressed up like the truth." The truth dried off; saw the lie's clothing, and refused to put them on. He decided to walk down the street with no clothes. People saw him and said, "There is the naked truth." God said in Psalm 101, that a liar would not tarry in His sight.

Ask the Lord to deliver you from people. Please God not man. Man will let you down. Man will anesthetize you. Do not allow man to talk you out of your inheritance. Realize that persecution occurs at various levels in our lives and strikes from a variety of sources. Did you know that regrets, guilt, and remorse can torture the soul? Choose to take a positive attitude toward persecution. Every man, woman, boy or girl must take a stand for what he believes and run the risk of rejection and/or ridicule.

Forgive those who have hurt you. Ask God for His divine intervention. Jesus said, in Luke 23:34a: *"Father, forgive them; for they know not what they do."* Trust God to do what you ask of Him. Allow Him to turn persecution into opportunities for forgiveness, caring for the sick, or simply showing love and compassion. Let me explain: You were created in the image and likeness of God. When you ask someone if they are having a good day and they respond no. Remind them, to appreciate and value what they don't think, they have. You can see that they have the activity of their limbs. Nonetheless, they seem to be saying to God, although I am physically well, it isn't enough. Ask yourself how often do we seem to disregard the blessings of the LORD. *"This is the day which the LORD hath made; we will rejoice and be glad in it."* (Psalm 118:24) Are you rejoicing? Who or what has stolen your joy?

Let your past go. Stop living in the past. Philippians 3:13-14 gives us a simple directive. *"Brethren, I count not myself to have apprehended: but this one thing I do, forgetting those things which are behind, and reaching forth unto those things which are before, I press toward the mark for the prize of the high calling of God in Christ Jesus."* God has a plan for your life. Renew your mind and thoughts with the Word of God. Remember, "As a man thinks in his heart so is he." Speak words out of your mouth that line up with the Word of God. God and His Word are inseparable. Declare His Word in season and out of season. Eat sleep and drink the Word of God. "It is a lamp unto your feet and a light unto your pathway." Decree and declare, who you are, in accordant to the Word of God.

You Are A King's Kid

Do you know who you are? You are a King's Kid. You are made in the image, and likeness of Almighty God. He is your righteousness. You are fearfully and wonderfully made. You are anointed with the burden removing, yoke destroying power of Almighty God. He is in control of every facet of your life. You have such an anointing on your life. God is always there in the personage of the Holy Spirit walking you through every situation. Although you are "*Living In A Glass House*," put your trust in God.

Jesus promised never to leave you nor forsake you. He promised to be with us until the end of the world. I am so glad about it. Aren't you? I want to encourage you to put your *"Trust in the LORD with all thine heart; and lean not unto thine own understanding. In all thy ways acknowledge Him, and He shall direct thy paths."* (Proverbs 3:5-6) It takes one word from God to change your situation. It takes one word from God to change you in the midst of your situation. Nothing you do can replace the time you spend alone with God. Take the limits off of Him.

You must renew your mind with the Word of God. His Word is a lamp unto your feet and a light unto your pathway. Get away from feeling sorry for yourself. Woe is me for I am undone should not be a part of your life. Poor me, nothing is ever going right for me. Remove from your mindset. Everybody is against me. There is nothing I can do to change my plight. I encourage you to stay away from every evil thought. Stop feeling sorrow for yourself. You need to eat, sleep, love and live. *"Casting down imaginations, and every high thing that exalteth itself against the knowledge of God, and bringing into captivity every thought to the obedience of Christ;"* (II Corinthians 10:5)

Stop the endless mind chatter. Begin to release words out of your mouth that will establish who you are in Christ Jesus. Speak the Word of God with wisdom, boldness and authority. The words that you speak are spirit and life. Watch what you say out of your mouth. Meditate upon the living Word of God. Do the Word on a daily basis. Plant it in your heart that you might not sin against God. Always study the Word. Begin the process of seedtime, and harvest. Get involved in seedtime, and harvest. Pray in the

Spirit for clear concise directions. *"But ye, beloved, building up yourselves on your most holy faith, praying in the Holy Ghost,"* (Jude 20)

Plant Righteous Seeds

Remain consistently committed to what you plant and walk in it. Expect to reap a bountiful harvest on the seed that you sow. My Mom always told us that we would reap what we sow. Take a principle; operate in it consistently to receive a breakthrough. That principle is found in Galatians 6:7. *"Be not deceived; God is not mocked: for whatsoever a man soweth, that shall he also reap."* When you sow seed, it will produce a bountiful harvest. When bad or good seed is sown, you will reap that harvest. If you desire a breakthrough in your life, work the principle until something positive materializes for you. If things are happening in your life that is not a result of the seeds you have sown, tell that devil, "I didn't sow these seeds, and I am not going to reap this harvest." You do not have to receive everything the devil throws your way. Resist the devil and he will flee from you. Resist him by not following his tactics nor distractions.

Delight yourself in the things of God. Be pliable, flexible, workable, obedient and loyal. Loyalty is changing your plans to accommodate someone else. How often do you change your plans to help someone other than yourself? When your heart is pliable, God can come in and direct His Will and Way in your heart. You can't stop an individual who knows that His God is with him. Put that individual in any situation and he will succeed.

"For they being ignorant of God's righteousness, and going about to establish their own righteousness, have not submitted themselves unto the righteousness of God." (Romans 10:3)

"For I say, through the grace given unto me, to every man that is among you, not to think of himself more highly than he ought to think; but to think soberly, according as God hath dealt to every man the measure of faith." (Romans 12:3)

"Therefore let no man glory in men. For all things are your's;" "And ye are Christ's; and Christ is God's." (I Corinthians 3:21, 23)

"For who maketh thee to differ from another? and what hast thou that thou didst not receive? now if thou didst receive it, why dost thou glory, as if thou hadst not received it?" (I Corinthians 4:7)

"Casting down imaginations, and every high thing that exalteth itself against the knowledge of God, and bringing into captivity every thought to the obedience of Christ;"
(II Corinthians 10:5)

"Let nothing be done through strife or vainglory; but in lowliness of mind let each esteem other better than themselves."
(Philippians 2:3)

"(For many walk, of whom I have told you often, and now tell you even weeping, that they are the enemies of the cross of Christ: Whose end is destruction, whose God is their belly, and whose glory is in their shame, who mind earthly things.)"
(Philippians 3:18-19)

"Not a novice, lest being lifted up with pride he fall into the condemnation of the devil." (I Timothy 3:6)

"For men shall be lovers of their own selves, covetous, boasters, proud, blasphemers, disobedient to parents, unthankful, unholy, Without natural affection, trucebreakers, false accusers, incontinent, fierce, despisers of those that are good, Traitors, heady, highminded, lovers of pleasures more than lovers of God; Having a form of godliness, but denying the power thereof: from such turn away." (II Timothy 3:2-5)

"Every good gift and every perfect gift is from above, and cometh down from the Father of lights, with whom is no variableness, neither shadow of turning." (James 1:17)

"But if ye have respect to persons, ye commit sin, and are convinced of the law as transgressors." (James 2:9)

"But he that received seed into the good ground is he that heareth the word, and understandeth it; which also beareth fruit, and bringeth forth, some an hundredfold, some sixty, some thirty."

-Matthew 13:23

May the God of all creation bless you with loving kindness, peace, joy, good health protection, strength and perpetual growth.

As you continue to sow seeds of righteousness: may God's eternal blessings always sustain you.

So watch your seeds germinate as you nurture and water them. May their yield forever bring forth good fruit in abundance. Amen. Amen.

How Committed Are You?

Chapter 10

Preachers' Kids, realize before you can complete anything you start, it requires commitment. How committed are you? Do you start multiple tasks, and do not finish them? How many uncompleted task do you have on your plate at this time? Are you committed to the very end? I encourage you to go all the way with the LORD. Set your face like a flint until you reach the end of the road. Prove God and watch Him come through for you and yours. You ask yourselves, "How can this thing work for me? What if I commit and fail?" Yes, it can and will work for you. Nothing beats a failure, but a try. Step out on the water and go to Jesus. It is time to get out of your comfort zone.

Stop retaking the chapter test. It is time for the mid-term and then the final. Speak life in your dry and dying places. Death and life are in the power of your own tongue. Choose to speak life. Decree the Word of God like Job. *"Thou shalt also decree a thing, and it shall be established unto thee: and the light shall shine upon thy ways."* (Job 22:28) What you decree shall be established, not might, perhaps or maybe. When you make your decree, *light shall shine* upon your path. What are you decreeing in your life today?

Do not back up, give up, cave in and/or quit. When you do, you doubt the truth of God's Word. Take God at His Word. Decree and declare in the name of Jesus, I am victorious. I can do all things through Christ who strengthens me. We often sing a song that says: *"In the name of Jesus, I have the victory; demons have to flee."* Total victory is realized when you stand on the unadulterated Word of God from Genesis to Revelation. Stand on the Promises of God. Remind our Heavenly Father of His Word concerning us. We must believe to receive. God is faithful that promised. His love for us will bring it to pass. Simply be still and know that God is God. His Word works! If it doesn't work, you need to go on to something else. Aren't you glad to know that there are no flaws in the things of God? You cannot find any discrepancies. God's Word works all by itself.

I am here to tell you that it works. Just take a stand for right and righteousness. *"But my God shall supply all your need according to His riches in glory by Christ Jesus."* (Philippians 4:19) Tenacity must rise up in you. Always know that God can and will supply all your needs. If you are to doubt anything, doubt your doubts not God. How do you know what God can and will do? The answer can be found in the Word of God. Search the Scriptures daily for in them you have life and they do testify of the Authenticity and Divinity of our Lord and Savior Jesus Christ. Deposit on the inside of you the experience of victorious living. As you study the Bible, question if you have deposited that experience within your heart, soul, mind, body and spirit. Meditate on the Word of God. Think deep on God's Word. Dissect the Word of God. Analyze the Word. Apply God's Word. Get a promise from the Bible and stand on it. God's Word is forever settled in heaven. It is alive. It is quick, powerful and sharper than a two-edged sword. It goes directly to the root cause of your issues when it is applied. God's Word is good for what ails you, physically, mentally, emotionally, socially, financially, and even materially.

The more incompletes you have, the more questions and doubts consume you. You will experience having burdens removed and yokes destroyed because of the anointing as you become saturated in God and His Word is in you. The Holy Spirit is telling you to go ahead, step out on the water and go to Jesus. When you do this, nothing shall be impossible for you. Jesus was committed to die on the cross for you and me. He would not be deterred. He was committed to realizing the resurrection experience. Be encouraged to stay committed to God and His Word. Keep going. Do not stop. No matter what you hear, keep going. Do not allow negativity to stop you from reaching your desired end. Jealous people are on the bottom trying to bring you down to their level. Do not let that happen.

God wants to get you into a place where He can speak to you. He is committed to you. Seek His face. God desires intimacy with you. Learn who your Heavenly Father is. Get a personal relationship with Him through our Lord and Savior Jesus Christ. God is in love with you. Let me say that again. *God is in love with you.* He hates your sin but He loves you so every much. Stop lying on God. He is not punishing you. His presence can't indwell you or come upon you when you are practicing and living in sin. Accept Jesus as Lord; and make a commitment to serve Him.

All God wants from you is YOU. Take care of the body God has given you. He is standing with His arms wide open asking you to come into His presence. *"Behold, I stand at the door, and knock: if any man hear My voice, and open the door, I will come in to him, and will sup with him, and he with Me."* (Revelations 3:20) What bothers you, bothers Him. Do not push Him away from you. He desires to be involved in every facet of your life. Jesus requests in Matthew 11:28: *"Come unto me, all ye that labour and are heavy laden, and I will give you rest."* You can always find rest in the presence of Almighty God. In His presence is fullness of joy and at His right hand are treasures forever more. You can cease from all of your worrying. Simply, put your trust and confidence in God.

Restoration

Is there anything missing in your life? This is your day of restoration. You can be restored back to your place in God. Trust Him. God loves you so much with an everlasting love. He has drawn you unto Himself with loving kindness. In God's presence, the restoration process can be completed. What is restoration? Restoration is putting back what was missing in your life. It is a return, total restitution. God assures us in Joel 2:25-26: *"And I will restore to you the years that the locust hath eaten, the cankerworm, and the caterpiller, and the palmerworm, my great army which I sent among you. And ye shall eat in plenty, and be satisfied, and praise the name of the LORD your God, that hath dealt wondrously with you: and my people shall never be ashamed."* Restoration is available to all of us. The time of total restoration is here. Rejoice!This is your Restoration Day. When I think of absolute restoration, I think of the prodigal son described in Luke 15:11-32. He returned home from another country, having eaten from the pens of swine. Yet, his Father received him back home. He put on him the best robe. He put a ring on his hand, and shoes on his feet. His Father gave him something he didn't expect on that day of return – compassionate love and forgiveness.

The prodigal son decided he wanted all of his inheritance. His father gave him his portion, and off he went. He spent all of his inheritance on riotous living. This young man ended up in the hog pen. He was eating the corn hulks from the swine when he came to himself. What a day of restoration that was for the prodigal son, and his family? When his father saw him coming down the road, things began to change in that household. That Father immediately had a celebration. The son that he thought was gone had come back home. He received total restoration back to his place in the family. His Father was delighted that the son who was lost had finally returned. God is like the like the Father of the prodigal son. He desires to restore you back to your place in Him. God has given us many good and precious promises in His Word. Thus, by faith, you can experience that God and His Word are inseparable.

Your day of restoration is the day the LORD rolls away the shame and disgrace of your past. He is waiting for you to return home. You left home. Will you come back home, today? It is easy to do. Simply, repeat this prayer with me:

> "God be merciful to me, a sinner. Forgive me for my sins. Wash me in the Blood of the Lord Jesus Christ. Save my soul and write my name in the Lamb's Book of Life. I come to You in the Name of Jesus." Amen. Amen.

Reflections: In Retrospect

Chapter 11

Midway Musings

Here we are at Chapter Eleven. Reflections: In Retrospect. We have come to the midpoint of my book; Preachers' Kids: Living In Glass Houses. First, after completing the front matter: that is, the title page through the preface, we began our subdivision journey with Chapter One: Our Only Wish Is To Be Normal. Our hearts cried out a simple wish to be normal. Our desire is to be known and seen as ordinary men, women, boys and girls. But, what does it mean to be normal? What is it like to be considered ordinary, regular, or simply just like everyone else? Albeit, we have discovered that we share a unique normalcy. We are Preachers' Kids! Although, we may not be seen as typical, nor should we be thought of or seen as "the worst kind."

We are all human. None of us have acquired angels wings. In essence, we are individuals who desire, want, need and deserve love, acceptance and understanding. So this intent is the premise of my book. Hence, our journey has brought us to Chapter Two: Accept Me For Me!!! Let Me Be Me!!! Stop trying to make us into images of our Parents and/or Guardians. They are God's Leaders, serving in humanity's limelight. But, we would like to be allowed space to find our own place in this world. This is the sincere desire of our hearts. However, not many people care to hear about our challenges. They have their own lives, and we should be content as the posterity of Leadership. Yet, we need to be accepted as normal individuals, simply living and enjoying life.

Next, we moved on to Chapter Three: How Do You See Yourself? Here, we are required to do some self-review evaluations. You will discover various ways to do introspection. We talk about issues such as: What do you desire of the Lord? Are you making excuses for not going forward with God? The spotlight was shone on you, your life and where you live. You were queried about how you really see yourself? We had a personal conversation. This heart-to-heart talk helped us to be true and honest to and with ourselves. As things evolved, you opened up, and criticized us for being "the worst kind."

Our traveling takes us through Chapter Four: The Worst Kind of What? This is our primary focus and directional point. We are frequently rebuked for being the "worst kind" and for our lack of living up to our Parents standards. We seem to be under close scrutiny all the time. It is the onlookers who tend to determine our brand. Our lives appear to be constantly under their microscope. We feel as though we are "living in glass houses." When will it end? Or more significantly, will the faultfinding offspring-watch ever stop? Being often referred to and/or suspect of being so awful will tend to wear your spirit down. Negative accusations and propaganda often hurled around about Preachers' Kids can cause much undue pain and suffering. Pain hurts, no matter who the recipients are, and/or what the situation. Constant negative finger-pointing such as:

- Did you see what she wore to the wedding? How could her Parents let her go out like that?
- His Parents allowed him to come to Church without a tie. He also had his shirt-tail out. He should have known better.
- I thought I heard him/her curse the other day. The things young people say these days.

And the probing conversations run on and on. Albeit, you may try to be model citizens, yet you are still culpable. If you are radical, you are amiss for making your Parents ashamed due to your behavior. It appears that someone is always trying to find fault to bring you down to size. Nevertheless, be encouraged. Do not allow anyone or anything to run interference on your relationship with God and cause you to miss your blessing.

Here we are at Chapter Five: Forgive The Offenders. So as you make the decision to stay the course with God, know that total forgiveness is the key to a vivacious Christlike life. To overcome and defeat the adversary, you must forgive the offender [off-ender]. Our Lord and Savior, Jesus

Christ told us in John 10:10: *"The thief cometh not, but for to steal, and to kill, and to destroy: I am come that they might have life, and that they might have it more abundantly."* Dear Reader: In Christ, we can live life in fullness, until it overflows. Simply, decide to be yourself. Love you for you. Realize how special you are to God. There is no one on earth like you; past, present, or in the future. You were made in the image and likeness of God, our Father. Hence, no other person's opinion can destroy your life if you refuse to believe, and accept their persuasive message. *"Casting all your care upon Him; for He careth for you."* (I Peter 5:7)

Our steady trek has brought us to Chapter Six: "To Every Thing There Is A Season." Seasons. Seasons. Seasons. Seasons. Ecclesiastes 3:1 tells us: *"To every thing there is a season, and a time to every purpose under the heaven:"* Although seasons change; yet, in the appropriate season, seeds are planted, nourished and cultivated. Then, in their proper season, we witness the fruit of them. From year to year, we reap a varied harvest. Most times, the yield is excellent and gratifying. Yet, every once in a while, the harvest is scarce, and/or unproductive. Yet, seeds of every kind are again sown in faith, with expectation of a rich harvest. Seasons. Seasons. Seasons. Seasons. How they change. Look at this: Apostle Paul was keenly aware of the change in seasons. In Titus 3:12-14: He wrote *"When I shall send Artemas unto thee, or Tychicus, be diligent to come unto me to Nicopolis: for I have determined there to winter. Bring Zenas the lawyer and Apollos on their journey diligently, that nothing be wanting unto them. And let our's also learn to maintain good works for necessary uses, that they be not unfruitful."* God desires His people to maintain fruitful works for the Kingdom of God, in and out of season. Amen. Amen.

In addition, be ever alert, be cognizant and aware of your surroundings. The adversary will attempt to use any one and/or any thing possible to side track and/or hinder your successful progress.

Do not allow distractions, nor frustrations to delay or restrain your progress and development in Christ. I Peter 5:8 advises us to: *"Be sober, be vigilant; because your adversary the devil, as a roaring lion, walketh about, seeking whom he may devour: Whom resist stedfast in the faith, knowing that the same afflictions are accomplished in your brethren that are in the world."* As a result, be careful to take earnest heed to watch and pray. Always be cognizant of the enemy's tactical mirages. The adversary seeks to devour God's people, regardless of who they are, where they live, etc. So do not allow the adversary to sneak up on your blind side. Thus, this is our lead into Chapter Eight: Recognizing Enemy Tactics.

Do you know who the enemy [adversary] is? Should you be concerned about an unseen enemy? I can hear the wheels turning in your mind now. You tend to blame every one and every thing for life's challenges. But know that: *"The Lord is my shepherd; I shall not want."* (Psalm 23:1) So stop pointing fingers and blaming yourself, and/or others for life's blunders. Rather, check your place in God. Give yourself to prayer and Bible study. Always know that God loves you, and is always with you. He promises never to leave you, nor forsake you. Therefore, no problem can break you unless you sign for it. Salvation is free, but it isn't cheap. The price was *paid in full* by the blood of our Lord and Savior Jesus Christ. That priceless blood is too precious to be considered cheap. Rather, it is a gift of love. All we are required to bring is, believing faith, in the Lord Jesus Christ. Now we leave receiving God's love gift of redemption. So why are you relinquishing your faith in God to fear of the adversary? Again, Psalm 23:4 says *"Yea, though I walk through the valley of the shadow of death, I will fear no evil: for thou art with me; Thy rod and Thy staff they comfort me."* Cancel giving heed to the enemy's fear and discouragement.

Did You know?

Do you know that your words have power? We ought to ask the LORD to set a watch, before our lips. We need Him to keep the doors of my mouth close. Dear Reader, always watch what you say. Did you not know that death and life is in the power of your own tongue, not someone else tongue, but your own tongue. *"Death and life are in the power of the tongue: and they that love it shall eat the fruit thereof."* (Proverbs 18:21) Are you speaking death or life over your own life? What about the lives of your family, friends, your community, America, and/or the world? We are admonished in Holy Scripture to choose life that we shall live. Watch those conversational words that people often say in agreement with others, without understanding the potential consequences of what is being said. Yet, we are making verbal agreements all the time. Matthew 18:19

reminds us: *"Again I say unto you, That If two of you shall agree on earth as touching any thing that they shall ask, it shall be done for them of my Father which is in heaven."*

You may say, I have "freedom of speech." I can do and/or say any thing I want to, as long as I don't hurt anybody. Hence, we pretty much say what we will and make noxious statements such as:

- If it is not one thing, it is another.
- I almost laughed myself to death.
- This thing is killing me.
- You are no good.
- Your daddy was nothing; your mom was nothing and you and your children will never be nothing.
- I feel like a dog.
- I wish this or that calamity . . . we go on and on talking, talking . . . barely giving thought to what we are saying.

Always, check your words. Put a bridle on your tongue. What are you saying? What have you been speaking out of your mouth? Let's stop the insanity. Dear Reader, enough with loose careless talk. It is time to make a fresh verbal start. Why not let today become our new word-sentinel beginning. Psalm 150:6 encourages us to praise the LORD. *"Let every thing that hath breath praise the LORD. Praise ye the LORD."* So as long as we are breathing, let's watch what you say, and when we don't know what to talk about, simply, lift your mind and heart to God in praise. Simply take the mask off; look at yourself. Appreciate what God has done in your life and live!

Our journeying has brought us here to Chapter Nine. Preachers' Kids: Let's Talk. So let's talk about life issues. Here, a brief conversation is in order. God is speaking to your heart. He is sending you messages from His Word, the Holy Bible. Are you listening? Do you hear what He is saying to you? Listen! Listen! Listen to your messages! God wants you to be made whole. He wants your heart filled with joy unspeakable and full of glory.

Stop trying to please man. Do you know who you are? Let me remind you. You are a King's kid. You are a Royal Priesthood, a called out nation, a peculiar people. When you speak words out of your mouth, speak words of life, righteous words of faith. Remember, by the words you speak you can be justified and/or condemned. We must speak faith-filled words out of our mouths. Words have tremendous power.

The words I AM are the most powerful in the universe. God gave these words to Moses. *"And Moses said unto God, Behold, when I come unto the children of Israel, and shall say unto them, The God of your fathers hath sent me unto you; and they shall say to me, What is His name? what shall I say unto them? And God said unto Moses,* I AM THAT I AM: *and He said, Thus shalt thou say unto the children of Israel, I AM hath sent me unto you."* (See Exodus 3:13-14) And so, these five words are precise and very powerful. Do not combine or connect negative words with I AM. These are the words that God used to introduce Himself to Israel. Why should we defile these words with destructive negativity?

Get in touch with the Holy Spirit on the inside of you. Trust Him to lead and guide you into all truths. He is the Paraclete, the one called to be with us as Teacher and Comforter, abiding with us forever. Simply trust God with your dreams, visions and plans for your life. Don't give up, or cave in nor give up and quit. You must fix your face like a flint. Make a decision to earnestly pray without ceasing. Eat, sleep and drink God's Word. It is a lamp unto our feet and a light unto our pathways. Rededicate your life to serving the True and Living God. Do as Isaiah 50:7 advises: *"For the Lord God will help me; therefore shall I not be confounded: therefore have I set my face like a flint, and I know that I shall not be ashamed."*

Here we are. Our journeying has brought us to Chapter Ten: How Committed Are You? Wow, this question is very bold and inquisitive. The title is asking a point blank question. How committed are you? Are you straddling the fence? Do you have a leg and a foot on each side? Are you double-minded and unstable in some of your ways? Do you desire to be restored? Restoration is here. However, do you want it? As we travel onward, know that God promises restoration. So while resting, take a little time to study and meditate in the Holy Scriptures. You will realize that Restoration is a blessed assurance from Almighty God. Joel 2:25-26 declares: *"And I will restore to you the years that the locust hath eaten, the cankerworm, and the caterpillar, and the palmerworm, my great army which I sent among you. And ye shall eat in plenty, and be satisfied, and praise the name of the Lord your God, that hath dealt wondrously with you: and My people shall never be ashamed."*

As we are traveling, I perceive more than ever, that the foundation of all things is to know that God IS God. Psalm 46:10 mandates: *"Be still, and know that I am God: I will be exalted among the heathen, I will be exalted in the earth."* God loves you for you. He is concerned about everything that concerns you. So it is time for us to focus on His will for our lives. Are you committed to God, and the things of God? Do you know what you want? It is time to take off the mask. Stop being pretentious. As a child you may have pretended to be something you were not. As an adult, it is time to face yourself and determine to be true to you. Stop being selfish and self-centered. Rather, become philanthropic, and learn how to provide Godly loving-kindness. As you face yourself, front, back and center, be restored back to the person God has called you to be. Thus, I remind you to always listen to the Holy Word of God, the Bible. God uses the Holy Spirit to impart His Words of Wisdom unto us. He promises to lead and guide us into all truths. Amen.

Can you believe it? We are now here at midpoint! We have journeyed through the front matter, continuing on from one chapter to the next. Finally, our trek has reached Chapter Eleven. Reflections: In Retrospect. Since we are at the end of an important midpoint in the book, let's peruse Words of Wisdom from my Mom, Mother Mary Ruth Bowens. [May her memory be blessed.]

> *"She openeth her mouth with wisdom; and in her tongue is the law of kindness. She looketh well to the ways of her household, and eateth not the bread of idleness. Her children arise up, and call her blessed; her husband also, and he praiseth her."*
> (Proverbs 31:26-28)

- A Prologue -

Mother Mary Ruth Bowens
(My Mom at 90 years young)

Dealing with Peers

My Mom's Dad was a Preacher. She was the oldest of five Children. Mom's peers compared their parents with Mom's Parents. They were envious of her and would take things from her, such as her lunch. Lunch would consist of meat, peas or beans, cake or pie in a tin pail. After they ate her lunch, they would laugh saying, "I am full." Her friends would say, "Oh, she is a good person. She won't do anything bad to any of you although you ate her lunch." They would poke fun at her because her father was a Minister and she didn't wear pants.

Question: While growing up, did you resent God, and/or the Church?

Answer: No. I received the Holy Ghost in the middle of a cotton field in the heat of the day. I went down to the Mercy Seat one day and the Holy Ghost came. That very day, I was filled with the Holy Ghost. I don't have a care in the world. I have cast all my cares on the LORD knowing He cares for me.

Words of Wisdom: My Mom

Mother Mary Ruth Bowens was a beloved Wife and a loving Mom. She was also an ardent Author; Historian; as well as a Preacher, Teacher, and Radio Co-Pastor with my Dad: the Bishop Bowens.

My Mom, During Her Life, Sharing Priceless Gems: I was nineteen years old when I married my late husband, Bishop George Law Bowens, Jr. I never talked back to my Parents. My Mom taught us, a smile will carry you a long way. I was an honor student in school and I won many Spelling Bees. Although I didn't finish high school, God blessed me abundantly. I knew more than a lot of my peers who graduated. They did not understand it. But, I was always reading and writing. My Parents took me out of school to help with my siblings, and chores on the farm. Older Children were always expected to help with everyday tasks and farm duties. I wasn't bitter. I did what was required of me. My mind was continually stimulated, because I loved to read. I would read the Word of God, as well as other books and the newspaper all of the time. In God's Word, the Bible, I found wisdom, knowledge and understanding. The Bible says, "If any of you lack wisdom, let him ask of God, that giveth to all men liberally, and upbraided not; and it shall be given him." (James 1:5) God will give you what you are in the need of. God always gives work; but not everyone has the same job.

I encourage you to repent for all of the wrongs you have done. Ask God to forgive you for your sins. Invite Jesus to come into your heart and become LORD and MASTER of your life. Take a 180 degree turn, not a 360 degree. A 360 degree turn means you have gone around in a circle. A 180 degree means you have changed your posture and position. You have dealt with the sin and decided to give up all to follow Jesus. Do yourself a favor and stop telling people your dreams and your secrets. They will envy you and try to hinder your receiving: *"The blessing of the LORD, it maketh rich, and He* [God] *addeth no sorrow with it."* Talk to them about your realities. Tell them that you were once on skid row, but God. You were a wretch undone, but God. You were too mean to live and afraid to die, but God. You once were lost, but God. Now you are found. You were blind, but God. Now, you can see. Hallelujah!!

Scriptures for Meditation

"For they are life unto those that find them, and health to all their flesh. Keep thy heart with all diligence; for out of it are the issues of life. Put away from thee a froward mouth, and perverse lips put far from thee. Let thine eyes look right on, and let thine eyelids look straight before thee." (Proverbs 4:22-25)

"For we wrestle not against flesh and blood, but against principalities, against powers, against the rulers of the darkness of this world, against spiritual wickedness in high places."

(Ephesians 6:12)

"Ponder the path of thy feet, and let all thy ways be established. Turn not to the right hand nor to the left: remove thy foot from evil." (Proverbs 4:26-27)

"For God hath not given us the spirit of fear; but of power, and of love, and of a sound mind." (II Timothy 1:7)

"Christ hath redeemed us from the curse of the law, being made a curse for us: for it is written, Cursed is every one that hangeth on a tree:" (Galatians 3:13)

"For the word of God is quick, and powerful, and sharper than any twoedged sword, piercing even to the dividing asunder of soul and spirit, and of the joints and marrow, and is a discerner of the thoughts and intents of the heart." (Hebrews 4:12)

"Seeing then that we have a great high priest, that is passed into the heavens, Jesus the Son of God, let us hold fast our profession."
(Hebrews 4:14)

"Looking unto Jesus the Author and Finisher of our faith; Who for the joy that was set before Him endured the cross, despising the shame, and is set down at the right hand of the throne of God."
(Hebrews 12:2)

ACTIVATING EVENT: It is time to change your posture and position. Renew your mind with the Word of God. Stop allowing situations and circumstances to stress you out. Remember this: No problem can break you unless you let it. You have to sign for it.

BELIEF: As a man thinks in his heart, so is he. What do you believe the LORD to do for you? What do you want from the LORD? Abraham believed God and it was counted unto Him for righteousness because He called those things, which be not as though they were.

CONSEQUENCE: There are consequences to your actions. Believe you receive and you shall have it. If you truly believe, you shall receive. When will you receive it? After you believe you receive it.

If you believe an event is stressful, it will be. If you believe it is not, it won't be. It is time to take the limit off of God. Let God be God in every facet of your lives. When you focus on an activating event in your mind, it will stress you out. You become very irritated and irrational. By magnifying a situation or circumstance in your mind, you are calm, and that calmness will remain.

Always find the good in a bad situation. See the Glass as half full not half empty. It is time to become an optimist not a pessimist. Romans 8:28 reminds us: *"And we know that all things work together for good to them that love God, to them who are the called according to His purpose."* Most stressful events can have multiple consequences. Hence, I Peter 5:7 advises: *"Casting all your care upon Him; for He [Jesus] careth for you."*

Make it your custom to perpetually focus on good things, whenever possible. Whatever your focus, it may come about in your life. According to Proverbs 23:7a: *"For as he thinketh in his heart, so is he:"* Philippians 4:8 gives us a clear directive for our thought form. *"Finally, brethren, whatsoever things are true, whatsoever things are honest, whatsoever things are just, whatever things are pure, whatsoever things are lovely, whatsoever things are of good report; if there be any virtue, and if there be any praise, think on these things."*

Keep your inner dialogue positive. Stop the mind chatter. Control negativity. Do not allow the enemy to build a nest in your mind. *"Casting down imaginations, and every high thing that exalteth itself against the knowledge of God, and bringing into captivity every thought to the obedience of Christ;"*

(II Corinthians 10:5)

Avoid the blame game. It is natural to blame outside sources; but it escalates stress. Your pointing the finger at others for what has happened in your life is not of God. You must take responsibility for your actions. Forgive the off-ender and the offense. *"For if ye forgive men their trespasses, your heavenly Father will also forgive you: But if ye forgive not men their trespasses, neither will your Father forgive your trespasses."*

(Matthew 6:14-15)

Many people are experiencing a great deal of stress because of pointing the finger at others. It is everyone's fault but my own. Stress will be eliminated when no one is blamed. For every action, there is a consequence. *"I, even I, am He that blotteth out thy transgressions for Mine own sake, and will not remember thy sins. Put Me in remembrance: let us plead together: declare thou, that thou mayest be justified."* (Isaiah 43:25-26)

Seek the face of God with your whole heart. Ask God to help you through your low and high points. When you go through the valley of the shadow of death, God is with you. Shift your focus forward to what is and can be changed by applying the Word of God. When your focus is changed, stress will be short-circuited. Line your life up with the promises of God from Genesis to Revelations. *"And be not conformed to this world: but be ye transformed by the renewing of your mind, that ye may prove what is that good, and acceptable, and perfect, will of God."*

(Romans 12:2)

Keep every situation or issue in perspective. Put all issues aside at the end of the day. Cast all your cares and concerns upon God. Do not worry about anything. Give it over to the Lord and let Him work it out. See every situation afresh in the morning. *"Remember ye not the former things, neither consider the things of old. Behold, I will do a new thing; now it shall spring forth; shall ye not know it? I will even make a way in the wilderness, and rivers in the desert."* (Isaiah 43:18-19)

Pray over whatever comes your way. Nothing is too big or too small for my God. Don't sweat the small stuff that the devil throws your way. It is all small stuff because Jesus promised never to leave you nor forsake you. The question is, "If God be for you, who can be against you?" Psalm 43:5 asks: *"Why art thou cast down, O my soul? and why art thou disquieted within me? hope in God: for I shall yet praise Him, who is the health of my countenance, and my God."*

God loves you. He is concerned about every facet of your life. He doesn't want you to worry about anything. Philippians 4:8 tells us plainly what we should think on. *"Finally, brethren, whatsoever things are true, whatsoever things are honest, whatsoever things are just, whatsoever things pure, whatsoever things are lovely, whatsoever things are of good report: if there be any virtue, and if there be any praise, think on these things."* Things that are true, honest, just, pure, lovely, good reports; as well as virtue, praise, should be our focus and the center of our attention. We should confidently cast all of our cares on God, knowing that He cares for us. *"So that we may boldly say, The LORD is my Helper, and I will not fear what man shall do unto me."*

(Hebrews 13:6)

We must submit to God. Allow the Holy Spirit to lead and guide us into all truths. True submission to God is an act of confidence in Him. Trusting God and committing your life to His divine will produces action. It is not something we put on for convenience sake. James 4:7-8a advises: *"Submit yourselves therefore to God. Resist the devil, and he will flee from you. Draw nigh to God, and He will draw nigh to you."*

"WISDOM IS THE PRINCIPAL THING;
THEREFORE GET WISDOM; AND
WITH ALL THY GETTING GET
UNDERSTANDING."

Proverbs 4:7

The ISness of God

Chapter 12

"Thus saith the LORD, Let not the wise man glory in his wisdom, neither let the mighty man glory in his might, let not the rich man glory in his riches: But let him that glorieth glory in this, that he understandeth and knoweth me, that I am the LORD which exercise lovingkindness, judgment, and righteousness, in the earth: for in these things I delight, saith the LORD." (Jeremiah 9:23-24)

The ISness of God: Who is He to you? He may have healed some of you and you say, The LORD is my healer. I tell you that He is more than that. He put a roof over your head, so you say that The LORD is my shelter, but He is more than that. You may not have had a job and He gave you gainful employment. So you say The LORD is Jehovah-Jireh, my provider. Yes, He is that and so much more. Psalm 23:1 begins with *"The LORD is . . ."* After is, there are three dots to make it easy for you to understand. The LORD is whatever you need Him to be. That is who He is. You may have been in bondage to some sickness, disease or infirmity. God came in and delivered you. So you can truly say: The LORD is my Deliverer. He is the Lifter of my head, except He is better than that. When we were dead in sin, lost without hope and without help, God sent Jesus to die on Calvary's cross for our sins. He redeemed us back to Himself through the shed Blood of His Son, our LORD and Savior, Jesus Christ.

The LORD is Omnipresent – Everywhere Present at the same time. The LORD is Omniscient – All Knowing. The LORD is Omnipotent – All-Powerful. The LORD is the Lifter of my head. He is my Shelter in the time of a storm. He is my Food when I am *hungry. He is my Bridge over troubled waters. He is my Warhorse in the time of war. He is your Battle Axe in the time of battle. He is my Peace when I am troubled and I thank Him for that. He is everything to me, Hallelujah! I can tell you what God is for me, but you must make Him personal for you, because personal needs may differ from person-to-person. Whatever you need The LORD to be, anytime and anywhere: The LORD is to and for you. As well as, The LORD is to and for me. Hallelujah!*

"Thou wilt keep him in perfect peace, whose mind is stayed on Thee: because he trusteth in Thee. Trust ye in the LORD for ever: for in the LORD JE-HO-VAH is everlasting strength:"

(Isaiah 26:3-4)

It is my desire to remind you of why we are here and where we are going. We are to show loving kindness to mankind. The Scripture said *with loving kindness have I drawn you.* We are to distribute to the necessity of saints through love and service. We are taught as children to be given to hospitality or benevolence according to Romans 12:13. We care and want to serve one another as the LORD our God provides the means. Our responsibility is to serve God's people, and all humanity.

As Preachers' Kids, we must always remember the Great Commission. People are hurting. Many are in distress and pain. Countless members in the Body of Christ are in need of healing. Social Services' Ministries endeavor to meet the need of the whole man: be it spiritual, physical, emotional, social, material and/or financial. This restorative support helps to bring healing into a discernible effect.

Goals are very important. Keep your assignment ever before you. We need to focus on our charge given to us by the Almighty. Jeremiah 1:5, 8 proclaims: *"Before I formed thee in the belly I knew thee; and before thou camest forth out of the womb I sanctified thee, and I ordained thee a prophet unto the nations." "Be not afraid of their faces: for I am with thee to deliver thee, saith the LORD."* Examine yourselves. What are you doing? Write down your dreams and aspirations. Develop a steadfast Ministering Journal. Attend Workshops and Seminars to assist you in meeting your mission.

Preachers' Kids constantly touch the lives of people in our Churches, communities, cities and state in accordance with Matthew 25:40. *"And the King shall answer and say unto them, Verily I say unto you, Inasmuch as ye have done it unto one of the least of these My brethren, ye have done it unto Me."* As we allow the LORD to use each of us to meet people; we are rendering benefits and services as unto the LORD. As we do good for others, we are also healing ourselves. PKs, we are family. We are units of each other. We Are One!

The Bible provides wisdom, knowledge and understanding. So, what will cause Preachers' Kids, as well as Family members to develop a closer relationship with God? Walking in the Spirit is vital to discipleship. Leviticus 20:7 says: *"Sanctify yourselves therefore, and be ye holy: for I AM the LORD your God."* Prayer is talking to God. Studying God's Word is God talking to us. A good relationship with the LORD, requires us to spend time, in prayer and worship. Acting upon that can help revive every facet of our lives.

The Bible says in James 1:19-20: *"Wherefore, my beloved brethren, let every man be swift to hear, slow to speak, slow to wrath: For the wrath of man worketh not the righteousness of God."* You have two ears and one mouth. Hint? Listen more than you speak. Think about what you want to say before you say it. Be quick to listen and slow to speak. *"He that answereth a matter before he heareth it, it is folly and shame to him."* (Proverbs 18:13) When someone is speaking and you are anticipating what they are saying and cut them off, it is wrong and dishonorable. You are not in that person's mind to predetermine what he or she might say or do. Hear the conclusion of the whole thing before you answer and/or give an opinion.

You might say, what is communication then? It is to impart thoughts, opinions and information through words, deeds, and/or actions. It has to be successfully received, to be successfully communicated. Did you successfully communicate your message? To become a good communicator, one must first become a good listener. Others are not as interested in what we have to say as they are in what they want to say to us. Good communicators are determined by how well we listen – not how well we speak.

People want you to listen to them intently. Listen; just listen. Learn the art of listening and the value of using your tongue in a positive vain. Sometimes, WE TALK TOO MUCH! Learn to keep your mouths closed. The scripture says "And that ye *study to be quiet, and to do your own business, and to work with your own hands, as we commanded you; That ye may walk honestly toward them that are without, and that ye may have lack of nothing."* (I Thessalonians 4:11-12) *"In the multitude of words there wanteth not sin: but he that refraineth his lips is wise."* (Proverbs 10:19)

We can't talk and listen at the same time. God gave us two ears and one mouth. We should be able to listen twice as much as we speak. Self-centered behavior is always demanding to speak and refusing to listen. Root cause of most conflict in interpersonal relationships is people do not listen. Take the time to listen. One complaint of Preachers' Kids is my Parents do not listen to me. They listen to other people but never take time for me. I am tired of sharing my minister parent with other people. The question on the floor is? What is the key to communications? How do you communicate? Although you are talking, are you successfully communicating to others?

I am the Daughter of a Bishop and First Lady Bowens. My Parents taught me the difference between right and wrong. Dad set the example of a Godly man and Mom, that of a Godly virtuous woman of honor. My Dad was an empathetic; a Christ-like man of God. He went into the community, to the homes of members and non-members alike. He always shared the Good News of the Gospel, and Ministered to the need of the whole man. Dad was a loving and protective father. He would sit and tell us about life and the Word of God. He was a great communicator. In my hometown, Bishop Bowens was often characterized as the Preachers' Pastor.

The Bible describes a man who had an encounter with Jesus. John 5:2-9 reports the narrative this way: *"Now there is at Jerusalem by the sheep market a pool, which is called in the Hebrew tongue Bethesda, having five porches. In these lay a great multitude of impotent folk, of blind, halt, withered, waiting for the moving of the water. For an angel went down at a certain season into the pool, and troubled the water: whosoever then first after the troubling of the water stepped in was made whole of whatsoever disease he had. And a certain man was there, which had an infirmity thirty and eight years. When Jesus saw him lie, and knew that he had been now a long time in that case, He saith unto him, Wilt thou be made whole? The impotent man answered Him, Sir, I have no man, when the water is troubled, to put me into the pool: but while I am coming, another steppeth down before me. Jesus saith unto him, Rise, take up thy bed, and walk. And immediately the man was made whole, and took up his bed, and walked: and on the same day was the Sabbath."*

After laying around at the pool of Bethesda for thirty-eight years; one day the impotent man met Jesus. Whenever you meet Jesus, something will happen. What is your experience? Your Dad and Mom may have broken up. Nowadays, your Dad will not help you. You talk to the Pastor and say, "You do not know my situation." The question on the floor is: Do you want to get up? If you do, Jesus will help you get up. It doesn't matter how things look, or the circumstances; do you want to get up? Do you really want to get up? God is raising us up. "Then said He unto His disciples, The harvest truly is plenteous, but the laborers are few; Pray ye therefore the Lord of the harvest, that He will send forth laborers into His harvest." (See Matthew 9:37-38)

You must decide that you will not be last any more. Do you want to get up? No more excuses. No more talking. Let us get up and do something. Schools are closing while people are opening prisons all over the country. The prisons today are all state-of-the-art. Many schools have the same equipment for decades. The rich are likely to get richer, while the poor gets poorer. God has blessed us with life. I Timothy 6:6-8 encourages: *"But godliness with contentment is great gain. For we brought nothing into this world, and it is certain we can carry nothing out. And having food and raiment let us be therewith content."* Many people have a heart for Public Service: Be it urban, city, state, suburban and/or country. Do you desire to change? Wake up. You can implement change. Don't forget where you came from, or where you are going. Do you want to change? You need to do something affirmative for yourself. You are more dynamic than material possessions.

Man, how are you treating your wife? Woman, how are you treating your Husband? How are both of you treating your Children? Single persons, how are you treating yourselves? How are we all treating our Parents? Exodus 20:12 says:*"Honor thy father and thy mother: that thy days may be long upon the land which the LORD thy God giveth thee."* By the Grace of God, we [you] have the ability to rise up above any situation. The man by the pool of Bethesda had been in the same condition for years. Finally,

Jesus came by. He told Jesus all about his past. He could not fathom change. Jesus was there to change his deep-seated lingering disorder. When the man tried to get into the water, no one would help him. All he saw was dysfunction. You can't put your faith in man. Man will fail you. Can't anybody do you like Jesus? Once your perception accepts impairment as normal from your reality, then dysfunction becomes ordinary. However, it seems crazy, when dysfunction becomes normal and perception becomes your reality. Some come to see it as normal. No matter the situation, Jesus is always there for you.

Fruit of the Spirit

"But the fruit of the Spirit is love, joy, peace, longsuffering, gentleness, goodness, faith, Meekness, temperance: against such there is no law." (Galatians 5:22-23)

Love is the hammer. Joy is the electricity. When you need a jolt, plug into it. Peace is the walls. Long suffering is the foundation. Gentleness is the insulation. Meekness is the nails. Temperance is the plumbing. Faith is the bricks, purifying. The wise pig built his house out of bricks. The contractor is Jesus Christ. His natural dad was a carpenter named Joseph. Jesus wants to build your house and work out your situation. Let Him work it out, in you and for you. God has given you a vision. He will bring it to pass. *"Let us hold fast the profession of our faith without wavering; (for He is faithful that promised;)"* (Hebrews 10:23)

The Call of God

Chapter 13

I have called you for a Divine purpose to show My people, My love. You have been call to rebuild the old waste places; to root up, to tear down preconceived ideas about the LORD. The LORD has set before you an open door that no one can shut according to Revelation 3:8. Do not listen to the negativity around you. I am leading and guiding you in every situation. You are Mine. I love you. When you come into a situation, things change. You bring My presence. They act funny because they do not follow Me. Yes, some say they do but there is no personal relationship.

"Ye have not chosen Me, but I have chosen you, and ordained you, that ye should go and bring forth fruit, and that your fruit should remain: that whatsoever ye shall ask of the Father in My name, He may give it you." (John 15:16) My Son – My Daughter, I have chosen you. I love you. I want you to know that you were made in My image and likeness. I want what is best for you. You are an example of what I can and will do in the lives of someone who takes Me at My Word. Yield yourself to Me. I have brought you here for a reason and a purpose. You are on My assignment.

"Being confident of this very thing, that He which hath begun a good work in you will perform it until the day of Jesus Christ:" (Philippians 1:6) Open your mouth, I will speak for you. Don't be apprehensive about anything. I am in control of your life and your circumstances. You have been faithful over a few things. I will make you a ruler over many things. You are Mine. No one can pluck you out of My hands.

"The blessing of the LORD, it maketh rich, and He [God] *addeth no sorrow with it."* (Proverbs 10:22) I am supplying all your need; giving you the desires of your heart, blessing you above measure; making you the head and not the tail; a lender and not a borrower; above only; you shall never be beneath. I have blessed you above measure. Your name demands

favor; your silhouette demands favor; your voice demands favor and your person demands favor. No one can curse you. As Balaam tried to curse the Children of Israel and He could only bless them. Anyone that tries to curse you, can only bless you, because you are blessed and highly favored of the LORD.

Abraham's blessings are [ours] yours. God has overturned everything, every scheme of the enemy through His Son, Jesus Christ. Total restoration in all things belongs to all of us. So let go of the past; this is a new day. *"Remember ye not the former things, neither consider the things of old. Behold, I will do a new thing; now it shall spring forth; shall ye not know it? I will even make a way in the wilderness, and rivers in the desert."* (Isaiah 43:18-19) You are the apple of God's eye. He has promised never to leave you [us] nor forsake you [us]. If you can believe it; you can receive it. God has prepared a table before you [us] in the presence of your [our] enemies. Listen to Psalm 23:5: *"Thou preparest a table before me in the presence of mine enemies: thou anointest my head with oil; my cup runneth over."* Every hindrance has been removed. I Corinthians 2:9 reminds us: *"But as it is written, Eye has not seen, nor ear heard, neither have entered into the heart of man, the things which God hath prepared for them that love Him."*

Just relax in the LORD. "The joy of the LORD is your strength." Don't lean on your own understanding. Acknowledge the LORD in all your ways, and He will direct your path. Stop worrying. Cast all your cares upon the LORD for He cares for you. Delight yourself in the LORD. He will give you the desire of your heart. Remember, this is your season, your year of jubilee.

Father, open the eyes of my understanding so that I may know who I am in Christ. Teach me how to walk the way Jesus walked. Thank You Lord, for leading me by Your Holy Spirit. Thank You, for the power and the courage to do what You would have me to do. I pray in Jesus Name. Amen. Amen.

"So shall My Word be that goeth forth out of My mouth: it shall not return unto Me void, but it shall accomplish that which I please, and it shall prosper in the thing whereto I sent it." (Isaiah 55:11)

"There shall no evil befall thee, neither shall any plague come nigh thy dwelling. For He shall give His angels charge over thee, to keep thee in all thy ways." (Psalm 91:10-11)

"The angel of the LORD encampeth round about them that fear Him, and delivereth them." (Psalm 34:7)

"Who his own self bare our sins in his own body on the tree, that we, being dead to sins, should live unto righteousness: BY WHOSE STRIPES YE WERE HEALED." (I Peter 2:24)

"When the even was come, they brought unto him many that were possessed with devils: and he cast out the spirits with his word, and healed all that were sick: That it might be fulfilled which was spoken by Esaias the prophet, saying, HIMSELF TOOK OUR INFIRMITIES, AND BARE OUT SICKNESSES." (Matthew 8:16-17)

"Surely he hath borne our griefs, and carried our sorrows: yet we did esteem him stricken, smitten of God, and afflicted. But he was wounded for our transgressions, he was bruised for our iniquities: the chastisement of our peace was upon him; and with his stripes we are healed." (Isaiah 53:4-5)

"For the law of the Spirit of life in Christ Jesus hath made me free from the law of sin and death." (Romans 8:2)

"For though we walk in the flesh, we do not war after the flesh: (For the weapons of our warfare are not carnal, but mighty through God to the pulling down of strong holds;)" (II Corinthians 10:3-4)

"Put on the whole armour of God, that ye may be able to stand against the wiles of the devil. . . Above all, taking the shield of faith, wherewith ye shall be able to quench all the fiery darts of the wicked. And take the helmet of salvation, and the sword of the Spirit, which is the word of God:" (Ephesians 6:11, 16-17)

"He that dwelleth in the secret place of the most High shall abide under the shadow of the Almighty." (Psalm 91:1)

"He shall not be afraid of evil tidings: his heart is fixed, trusting in the LORD." (Psalm 112:7)

"And said, If thou wilt diligently hearken to the voice of the LORD thy God, and wilt do that which is right in his sight, and wilt give ear to his commandments, and keep all his statutes, I will put none of these diseases upon thee, which I have brought upon the Egyptians: for I am the LORD that healeth thee." (Exodus 15:26)

"See now that I, even I, am He, and there is no god with Me: I kill, and I make alive; I wound, and I heal: neither is there any that can deliver out of My hand." (Deuteronomy 32:39)

People have many unrealistic expectations of Preachers' Kids. We must be above reproach. They see us as miniature images of God because our Parent(s) are Ministers. There is always so much pressure to be perfect in the eyes of everyone who is aware of our status. Sometimes it seems that a sign is attached to you saying: "I should be perfect because I am a Preachers' Kid. Examine me. Put me under a microscope. See if I can measure up to what you expect a Preachers' Kid to do and be." You are a marked person who is expected to be better than most people If you are perceived as such, then you will be labeled as a snob or high echelon person. How can I ever measure up to what's expected of me? Can I be my own person with my own personality? Shall I try to imitate my Parents and/or or Grandparents?

What if I were not born a Preachers' Kids? I wish I didn't have to be something I can't live up to. How can I live up to your expectation of me? I am not perfect. It seems I am making more mistakes while trying to live up to your expectations. The pressure of being perfect is sometimes over whelming. It causes me to do things I would not have done if I were not looking for the approval of others. Yet, with faith in our hearts, we can never give up. Our Father God will get us where He has created us to achieve. We can always count on Him to get us there. Simply, Trust Him. Amen.

We are always held to a higher standard. This ought not be. Being judged by others should be taboo. We wish we didn't always have to be

Preachers' Kids

on display, because of who our Parents are. There is a stigma attached to Children of The Reverend Clergy. The status quo is this: You are held accountable because you are hanging out with the Preacher. They expect all Preachers' Kids to be like a little Jesus. We should behave the way Jesus probably behaved when He walked upon the earth.

Preachers' Kids, you may see people experimenting with various things, but you stay clear. You are held to a higher standard. Even sinners expect your life to be above reproach. While in college, one of my nieces attended a party on campus. When she arrived at the party, someone said to her. "What are you doing here? You know you do not belong here." She said she looked at her clothes and wondered if she was wearing a sign saying PK. Remember this, you are judged by the company you keep, the things you say, the clothes you wear and the things that you do. You are judged because you live in the same home with the Preacher. It is often said of you that if you can't get it right in the Preachers' home, how can anyone expect their Children to live the abundant life in Christ?

Minister Parents must let their Children know who they are and what is expected of them. They must encourage their Children to hold their heads up high. My Dad told us "Never let anyone put you down because of the color of your skin, what you have or do not have. You are as good as or better than anyone walking on two feet." Growing up in the segregated South, many challengers faced us. But the fact that my Dad was the Bishop and both Parents were Radio personalities, helped my siblings and me. We were not exposed to a lot of the racism because of our Minister Parents. Today, our Parents are still highly respected throughout the surrounding communities in South Carolina. Thank God for their righteous lives. They lived their testimonies. When any of us go home, we often hear people whispering, "that's Bishop and Mother Bowens children and/or grandchildren."

"LORD, Thou hast been our dwelling place in all generations. Before the mountains were brought forth, or ever thou hadst formed the earth and the world, even from everlasting to everlasting, Thou art God." (Psalm 90:1-2)

Just be the individual God made you. Don't try to measure up to the expectations of others. Know God is the keeper and not you yourself.

Remember Job? His perfection was not found in what he did but who he was. Do not live by the expectations of others but be all God wants you to be. Know God is watching and waiting for you. David made mistakes written in history but he had a heart that turned back to God. God called David, "A man after His own heart." David was quick to forgive and swift to repent for wrong doings. Don't allow past offenses to keep you away from God. He is waiting for you [for us] to repent and return to Him.

The Zealous Clergy

Chapter 14

God has called you into the Ministry of soul winning. He who wins souls is wise. In your zest to please God, you sometimes run ahead of Him. You may not always take time to adequately seek the face of God. Matthew 6:33 tells us: *"But seek ye first the kingdom of God, and His righteousness; and all these things shall be added unto you."* Did you seek the face of God? Are you studying to show yourself approved unto God? Are you rightly dividing, the Word of truth according to the Bible? II Timothy 2:15 admonishes us to:*"Study to shew thyself approved unto God, a workman that needeth not to be ashamed, rightly dividing the Word of truth."*

Someone told you or coerced you in believing that the Ministry comes first and you believed them. Why? *"Ye did run well; who did hinder you that ye should not obey the truth?"* (Galatians 5:7) Everyone and everything else is second. So, what did you do? Well, you quit your job without discussing it with your family. You said that it was done for the sake of the Ministry. Yet your family is suffering because of it. You insist that you had an epiphany in regard to leaving your job.

Did God make clear to you to suspend secular work? Otherwise, did people persuade you to quit? *YOU MAY HAVE THOUGHT YOU COULD WALK BEFORE YOU COULD CRAWL, SO YOU QUIT YOUR JOB.* Nevertheless, if you do quit your job, in spite of everything, always know that what God requires, He provides the enablement. Psalm 46:10 advises: *"Be still, and know that I am God: I will be exalted among the heathen, I will be exalted in the earth."* Having a discussion with your family, regarding the possibility of your quitting your job may bring more light to the conversation. Always look at the big picture. Consider all persons concerned. Whose lives may be affected by hurried decisions. Our God IS*!!* As an old song runs: "God is a Right Now God; YES HE IS*!* He May not Come When You Want Him, but He is Always Right on Time. He is a Right Now God; YES HE IS." May you and your family continue to be blessed as you seek the Lord in all your decisions. *"The LORD shall increase you more and more, you and your children. Ye are blessed of the LORD which made heaven and earth."* (Psalm 115:14-15)

Your attitude says GOD has called me, and I do not have to discuss my decision with any body. *I AM a man. I AM a woman. GOD has called me, and I will not let anyone stand in my way.* Then, there you are telling your family, along with everyone else, from the pulpit about your decision to quit your job. The LORD told me to quit my job and go into full time Christian service. I quit work on Friday. I gave them my notice. Friday was my last day. It doesn't matter to me what anyone thinks, I am being obedient to God and His call on my life. In the meantime, you are not providing for your family. They do not have the basic necessities. They are now suffering in silence. You feel justified as you go from place to place, trying to make do. Your family is suffering needlessly. You are causing them to resent God, and the things of God, by your actions.

When your Spouse comes to you to clear the air, you will not give her an ear to listen. You need to get rid of your selfish acts. Let go and let God. Go to your wife and Children. Ask them to forgive you. Pray that God will heal your relationship with the members of your immediate family. Tell your Wife how much you love her and need her help in the Ministry. This is not your Ministry alone. Tell your Wife and Children, it is our Ministry. We are in this together. I need you with me. I need your help. I can't do this alone. I need you or this may not work. You are important to me. The only person in front of your Wife is God. You must honor your Parents, respect your Wife, take care of your Children, and love God with all your heart, and your Neighbor as yourself.

Stop making your wife and Children feel like an after-thought. Let them know continually how important they are to you. Include them in all decision-making that will affect their lives. II Corinthians 2:11 inform us: *"Lest satan should get an advantage of us: for we are not ignorant of his devices."* Jesus cautions about three devices in John 10:10. He said: *"The thief cometh not, but for to steal, and to kill, and to destroy: I am come that they might have life, and that they might have it more abundantly."* Jesus came that we might have and enjoy life to the fullest until it overflows. Get your Family involved in conversation, and listen to their input. When you take heed to what they have to say; most opposition will be removed. Your Spouse is your Helpmate. Let her help you. You will receive favor from the LORD because of your Wife. *"Whoso findeth a wife findeth a good thing, and obtaineth favour of the LORD."* (Proverbs 18:22) You have given your attention beyond them. It is never too late to recant, nor change what has occurred. You can reach out to your Spouse, and Children now. Ask them to forgive you. Again, allow me to reiterate. While some of you are Ministering to the world, countless members of your Families are being forsaken, and/or feel that they are all alone.

Cultivate a relationship with them individually and collectively. It is never too late to show love to your Spouse and Children. Forgive yourself for not being there for them. Ask God to forgive you. Move forward in the love of Christ. Be encouraged to hug members of your Family, and spend quality time with them. Your Children will reciprocate when you reach out to them.

The Spouse

Tell your Spouse, God said in Genesis, chapter 2:24, *"Therefore shall a man leave his father and his mother, and shall cleave unto his wife: and they shall be one flesh."* However, you have behaved as though the two of you are separate. How can you repay her for your error? You can't compensate her by words only. You can only give back through deeds and actions. There is no payback. Genuine change can only be had, due to love and kindness. If you are willing to correct and fix what may have been broken over the years; God promises restoration.

God wants you to know that there is a Word for you in Joel 2:25-26: *"And I will restore to you the years that the locust hath eaten, the cankerworm, and the caterpillar, and the palmerworm, my great army which I sent among you. And ye shall eat in plenty, and be satisfied, and praise the name of the LORD your God, that hath dealt wondrously with you: and my people shall never be ashamed."* Demonstrate love and devotion to your Family. It is a Family Ministry. Go to your Family before going to God and ask them for forgiveness. Conversely, without God, it will not work.

Rev. Dr. Arnetha Bowens

The Offspring of The Reverend Clergy is in need of a total healing. This healing should include spiritual, mental, physical, social, financial, emotional and material. The hurts experienced are so deeply rooted and surrounded in fear. The enemy of your soul is trying to destroy you. It is time for you to face your hurts. Deal with self. Do you know who you are? It is time for you to *know* who you are. Take off the mask. First:*"To thine own self be true."* If you are not transparent with you, I know you will not be with anyone else.

The pain festering in your mind, body, spirit and life is not from God. The pain has brought fear. The fear brought you torment. Let us deal with the fear first. Psalm 23:4b says: *"I will fear no evil: for Thou art with me;"* I will fear no evil. Who is the Thou with you? Do you know who He is? He is Jehovah God, ELELYON. The Most High God is with you. I will fear no evil for Jesus is with me. I will fear no evil for the Holy Ghost is with me. I will fear no evil for Goodness and Mercy is following me. Jesus said, He will never leave me nor forsake me. He will be with me until the end. Therefore, I will fear no evil. Psalm 27:1 *declares: "The LORD is my light and my salvation; whom shall I fear? the LORD is the strength of my life; of whom shall I be afraid?"* II Timothy 1:7 instructs us: *"For God hath not given us the spirit of fear; but of power, and of love, and of a sound mind."*

Fear has torment. *"Casting down imaginations, and every high thing that exalteth itself against the knowledge of God, and bringing into captivity every thought to the obedience of Christ;"* (II Corinthians 10:5) Receive your healing today. Luke 9:11 shows kindness and compassion. *"And the people, when they knew it, followed Him: and he received them, and spake unto them of the kingdom of God, and healed them that had need of healing."* This is not just a physical healing. This is a total healing. Shalom – wholeness, nothing missing, nothing broken. Brokenness, lack, sickness, disease, infirmity, poverty, all come from the enemy of your soul. Wellness, wholeness, healing, prosperity and all good things come from God.

To the Offspring of The Reverend Clergy, let go and let God have His way in your lives. "But s*eek ye first the kingdom of God, and His righteousness; and all these things shall be added unto you."* (Matthew 6:33) Seek God's face, not His hands, with all your heart. Stop penalizing us because God called our Parent(s) into the Ministry. We are not perfect people, neither are our Parents. We shed tears, feel joy, pain, sorrow, excitement, as well as experiencing other emotions. The same sentiments that you feel, we feel. When we stand before the Bema Seat – Judgment Seat of Christ, we will all be judged the same. We are not perfect but we [mankind – those who accept Christ] are striving toward perfection.

Preacher: Stop trying to make your Children into angelic beings. They are flesh and blood Children. They may become angry, resentful and/or rebellious toward God, the Ministry and you. Do not allow outsiders to cause your Children unnecessary discomfort and pain. This will push them from God to serve the adversary, satan, who will use Church folk to provoke them to sin.

Your Children lives can be bruised due to your prideful thinking, that you have arrived. That spirit is not of God. Your behavior will judge you. Treating your Children with disdain and contempt, because of what people are saying, about their attitudes and actions are wrong. Why are you putting so much pressure on them? As a Minister, as quiet as it is kept, you are not perfect. All perfect people are home with the LORD. As my Dad once Preached, "*What Are You Doing When No One Is Looking?*" We are all red blooded individuals born into Preacher's Families. Some of us had stricter rules and regulations than others, but we are still PKs.

Parents accept your Children as they are. Encourage your Congregations to do the same. My Dad and Mom had weekly Family meetings with us to air our concerns. Daily, we were encouraged to be ourselves. We were not perfect but we were loved, encouraged and disciplined by Parents who were sold out to God; but they were not perfect people either. No one is perfect in their own strength. As long as we live in this flesh, it is an enemy of God.

Dad and Mom did not spare the Word of God nor the rod of correction. We were praised when we did well and were chastised when we didn't. They taught us God's Word at home and Church. We had Family Prayer and Family share time. We were not pushed into a Preaching Ministry, but we were always encouraged to love God with all our hearts and live exclusively for Him accepting Jesus as our LORD. When negative things were said by outsiders; Dad would nip it in the bud by explaining to us never to let anyone put you down for any reason because of what you do or do not have. You are as good as or better than anyone walking on two feet. *Let every man be a liar, but let God be true.* God's Word will stand forever. Dad loved us and we knew it. My Sisters and I were his Gals. And my Brothers were his Sons. He loved us and taught us to be the best we could be. He is at home with the LORD now, but we still speak very warmly of Dad's love and care for Mom and their Children. *May God Bless the Memory of Our Righteous Parents.*

As I write this book, my Mom is ninety years old. She is a virtuous woman of honor. She loves us and prays for us in season and out of season. Our precious Lady, an honorable woman of good reputation is the *love of our lives.* Dad always let Mom be her own person. She loves the LORD with all her heart. We were always encouraged to show love and kindness everywhere we went. *"Mom, I want to be like you when I grow up."* Our Parents lived honorable and Holy lives before us. We can go out into the world and show others the love of God because of Dad and Mom. They did not beat us over the head with the Bible. I thank God that they dealt with each of us at our own level of understanding. As a result, my siblings and I do not resent God, the Church or our Parents. We know God experimentally, through Godly teaching and Holy living by our Parents, in and out of our home. That made a difference in our lives. The opinions voiced by outsiders were not allowed to hurt us. It was like water on a duck's back. Dad was his own person; a man after God's own heart. Mom was a strong woman and his beloved Wife. We were his Children; their Children. Dad and Mom, together, made our house a home. Our environment was filled with love; a place where our Family, as well as so many others sought refuge. The love of God was shared with us, and with other people they came in contact with.

The breakdown is as follows: Dad, Mom and a Family of eleven Children. (May God bless the memory of those who are no longer with us). The three oldest Children died in early childhood. Eight of us grew up together: three Brothers and five Sisters. One Sister, a Missionary and Singer left us in August 1997. Her former Husband is a Deacon, a General Educational Development (GED) Instructor and a retired Law Enforcement Officer. Their Children are still dealing with the lost of their young Mom. Their Daughter is a brilliant Photographer. One Brother, a dynamic charismatic Preacher went home to be with the LORD in November 1998. He worked for a large TeleCom company assisting the deaf. He was also the Social Services' Director at a large Church. His Wife, now with the Lord, was a Phlebotomist. One of their Sons, an Engineer, is a Pastor/Missionary. Their other Son is an IT Entrepreneur.

Today, there are six of us: One Brother, a Bishop/Pastor is a retired Military Veteran. His wife is a Nurse. Their Children are super-talented. One Daughter is a Stationery and Print Designer. One Brother, a retired Metro Bus Driver, is an ordained Minister and a Musician. His Wife is retired Law Enforcement. Their Children are smart and talented. One Daughter is in the Military Reserves. One Sister is a Missionary and an exceptional Singer. Her late Husband was awarded a Purple Heart during the Vietnam War. Their Children are highly accomplished. One Daughter, upon graduating college, was inducted into the National Honor Society. One Sister, an amazing Singer, is a Healthcare Professional, BSN. Her Husband, a Vietnam-era Veteran, is a retired Law Enforcement Officer. Their Children are all high-achievers. One of their Daughters is a Military Physician. One Sister, an Education and Business Advocate, has a Law degree. Her late Husband was an ordained Minister. He volunteered as a Cleric to Community Hospitals, the Special Police, and those in need. Their Children are highly motivated to succeed. One Son is a successful Restaurateur. One Sister is me: The Reverend Doctor Arnetha Bowens. I am a Radio and Television Minister, and the Author of this book, "Preachers' Kids: Living In Glass Houses."

We are certainly blessed and honored to be PKs. The next generation are Artists, Authors, Clerics, College Professors, Doctors, Engineers, Entrepreneurs, Law Enforcement, Mechanics, Merchandisers, Musicians, Scholars, Teachers, etc. We are occupied in prayer, study, employment, and citizenship. We hope to do our part, in making this world a better place. While growing up in the South, our Parents worked tireless to make something of all of us. They loved us so much. We are so appreciative and indebted to their memory. Most of all, we are thankful to God for choosing righteous Parents for us. We could not have asked for better. There is no one better than they were. Praise the LORD. God has done great things, for us and through us.

They loved us, provided for us, sacrificed for us and trained us in the way we should go. God's Word is true. Now that we are older, we have not departed from their teaching. Although we are all adults, we are still in love with Jesus. *"Thy word is a lamp unto my feet, and a light unto my path."* (Psalm 119:105) We are not perfect, but God is sitting on the throne of our heart houses. We are growing daily in the things of the LORD. We are expecting God to daily; order our steps in His word. The Great Commission was given to everyone. God has called all of us [*mankind*] to go into all the world and [*be witnesses,*] preach the Gospel to every creature [*on* earth].

We often reminisce about our childhood and thank God for our training. Dad and Mom were Radio personalities for more than forty years. A few years ago, due to stress, Mom had a brain attack also known as a *stroke*. Since that time, I have taken some tiny steps in their shoes. I am presently carrying on their legacy on WJAY 1280 AM Radio in South Carolina, to the Glory and Honor of God our Father. What an honor and a privilege to be chosen by God, for such a time as this, to Preach the Good News of the Gospel of Jesus Christ. *To God Be the Glory for All He Has Done!!*

Who Are These People?

Chapter 15

These people, Preachers' Kids, feel like they are a forgotten group. Their Parents are out, evangelizing the world, while many of them have gone astray. Many have lost sight of God and the things of God. They are feeling ostracized, rejected, detested, unloved and unwanted. There is a battle going on in their minds to do evil and not good. The Fact: Parents are busy saving the world; while not taking an active interest in the needs of their children. Fact: Ministry activities and events create a perception of disregard and neglect. This can cause resentment of God, the Church, the Synagogue, the Temple, as well as the things of God.

A portion of this group has turned to lives of crime, drugs, dropped out of society and some have even committed suicide. Yes, suicide. Many individuals in this group are practicing their Parents' faith mechanically. Yet, some are actually living the life they sing and talk about – devotion to the Only True and Living God, Jehovah Jirah, ADONAI, YHWH, ELELYON – The Most High God. We need to encourage and strengthen the Children of The Reverend Clergy, letting them know first and foremost that they are not alone. Help them to get in touch with their feelings – be it love, anger, resentment, jealousy, envy, strife, joy, peace, goodness and/or happiness. We all need to be motivated to do and to be all we can. When we realize that the sky is the limit: our trust in God is able to grow, from "faith to faith." This group needs to be encouraged to turn back to God. He did not let them down. God loves each and every one of them. *"Casting all your care upon Him; for He careth for you."* (I Peter 5:7)

Teach them to look for the good in what seems to be a bad situation. Help them to see the glass half full rather than half empty. Focus on the good or positive things in life. God's word teaches us how to think. It reads: *"Finally, brethren, whatsoever things are true, whatsoever things are honest, whatsoever things are just, whatsoever things are pure, whatsoever things are lovely, whatsoever things are of good report; if there be any virtue, and if there be any praise, think on these things."* (Philippians 4:8) Avoid the blame game. It escalates stress. Keep inner dialogue positive. Always maintain a positive mental attitude. "[Y]et *will I not forget thee. Behold, I have graven thee upon the palms of My hands; thy walls are continually before Me."* (Isaiah 49:15c-16)

Offspring of The Reverend Clergy, God has us always on His mind. Many are in dire need of a total healing. This healing should include, but not be limited to spiritual, mental, physical, social, financial, emotional and material needs. The hurts and suffering can be so deeply rooted. Pain can become surrounded with anxiety and fear. Fear has torment. *"For God hath not given us the spirit of fear; but of power, and of love, and of a sound mind."* (II Timothy 1:7)

Face YOUR Hurts

The enemy of your soul is trying to destroy you. It is time to face all of those hurts. Deal with your self. Get to know who you are *and most of all whose you are.* By all means, take off the mask. First: *"To thine own self be true."* The pain festering in your mind, body, spirit and life is not of God. The pain you are experiencing has brought you fear. The fear has brought you torment. It is time to let go and let God have His way in you. Are you up for the challenge?

First, let's deal with your fears. Psalm 23:4 says: *"Yea, though I walk through the valley of the shadow of death, I will fear no evil: for Thou art with me; Thy rod and Thy staff they comfort me."* I will fear no evil. Who is the Thou with you? Jehovah God is with you. I will fear no evil for Jesus is with you. *I* will fear no evil for the Holy Spirit is always with me. I will fear no evil for the twins of goodness and mercy are following me all the days of my life. *"Surely goodness and mercy shall follow me all the days of my life: and I will dwell in the house of the LORD for ever."* (Psalms 23:6) Jesus said: *"He would never leave us nor forsake us."* Our Lord Jesus Christ is with us now and for ever. (See Hebrews 13:5-6)

I will fear no evil. *"The LORD is my light and my salvation; whom shall I fear? the LORD is the strength of my life; of whom shall I be afraid?"*

(Psalm 27:1) *"For God hath not given us the spirit of fear; but of power, and of love, and of a sound mind."* (II Timothy 1:7) *"There is no fear in love; but perfect love casteth out fear: because fear hath torment. He that feareth is not made perfect in love."* (I John 4:18) There is nothing but agony and torment in fear. God's unconditional love is essential for absolute peace.

It is virtually without adequate language for me to express the importance of God's way of thinking. II Corinthians 10:5 tells us: *"Casting down imaginations, and every high thing that exalteth itself against the knowledge of God, and bringing into captivity every thought to the obedience of Christ;"* Jesus healed them that had need of healing. By faith, receive your healing today. *"And the apostles, when they were returned, told Him all that they had done.*

And the people, when they knew it, followed Him: and He received them, and spake unto them of the kingdom of God, and healed them that had need of healing." (Luke 9:10a, 11) Jesus always had compassion on those that followed Him. He healed them. He encouraged them. He fed them. He always cared about the needs of the people. How do you care for yourself and others?

Today, I speak Shalom: completeness, wholeness (nothing missing, nothing broken) over you life. Brokenness, lack, sickness, disease, infirmity and poverty come from the adversary – the enemy of your soul. Love, joy, wholeness, healing, wellness, kindness, abundance, wealth and prosperity come from God. Believe and know that the LORD is your Shepherd and you shall not want.

Offspring of The Reverend Clergy: Let go and let God. Seek God. Matthew 6:33 advises: *"But seek ye first the kingdom of God, and His righteousness; and all these things shall be added unto you,"* Seek His face with all your heart. I encourage you to read and commit to memory Psalm 27 in its entirety. Make it your own. Spiritually insert your name in there, and your family members, as well as other loved ones.

Psalm 27

"The LORD is my light and my salvation; whom shall I fear? the LORD is the strength of my life; of whom shall I be afraid?

When the wicked, even mine enemies and my foes, came upon me to eat up my flesh, they stumbled and fell.

Though an host should encamp against me, my heart shall not fear: though war should rise against me, in this will I be confident.

One thing have I desired of the LORD, that will I seek after; that I may dwell in the house of the LORD all the days of my life, to behold the beauty of the LORD, and to enquire in His temple.

For in the time of trouble He shall hide me in His pavilion: in the secret of His tabernacle shall He hide me; He shall set me up upon a rock.

And now shall mine head be lifted up above mine enemies round about me: therefore will I offer in His tabernacle sacrifices of joy; I will sing, yea, I will sing praises unto the LORD.

Hear, O LORD, when I cry with my voice: have mercy also upon me, and answer me.

When thou saidst, Seek ye My face; my heart said unto Thee, Thy face, LORD, will I seek.

Hide not Thy face far from me; put not Thy servant away in anger: Thou hast been my help; leave me not, neither forsake me, O God of my salvation.

When my father and my mother forsake me, then the LORD will take me up.

Teach me Thy way, O LORD, and lead me in a plain path, because of mine enemies.

Deliver me not over unto the will of mine enemies: for false witnesses are risen up against me, and such as breathe out cruelty.

I had fainted, unless I had believed to see the goodness of the LORD in the land of the living.

Wait on the LORD: be of good courage, and He shall strengthen thine heart: wait, I say, on the LORD."

The Vision

"I will stand upon my watch, and set me upon the tower, and will watch to see what He will say unto me, and what I shall answer when I am reproved. And the LORD answered me, and said, Write the vision, and make it plain upon tables, that he may run that readeth it. For the vision is yet for an appointed time, but at the end it shall speak, and not lie: though it tarry, wait for it; because it will surely come, it will not tarry. Behold, his soul which is lifted up is not upright in him: but the just shall live by his faith."
(Habakkuk 2:1-4)

We should rehearse God's history. It re-affirms our faith. While it is time consuming, spend time with God. Spend time with God in the midst of your pain and suffering. Forget the impossibilities. Let God's Word resonate in your heart. You might say: God, it looks impossible; but so did the Red Sea. God, it looks so impossible; but so did the Walls of Jericho. LORD, it may look unattainable; but so did occupying the Promised Land. God has done great and mighty things for us. If you were to check Genesis through Revelations – the half has never been told. Spend time seeking God's face. Let Him put His purpose into your heart.

God sent the east wind and backed up the Red Sea. More than six million Jews walked across on dry ground. What a Miracle? There was not a feeble one among them. Not any of them got a splash on them. If God did that then; He can do it now. When you are struggling with situations and/or circumstances wondering how God will come through for you; look back at His history. Then, look forward through Faith to His Grace and Mercy. Can God do what He said? Is He able to do what He promised? If God has promised to do something, you can Trust His Word as recorded in Scripture.

It doesn't matter what your situation may be, *Give Thanks* and *Praise to God*. II Thessalonians 5:18 says: *"In every thing give thanks: for this is the will of God in Christ Jesus concerning you."* When you open your mouth, and begin to lift up the Name of Jesus, you will begin to understand why He sent the rain and the storm. When it seems that your blessing was held back; God never forgets! God is an on-time God. All He desires from us is a living testimony. People are watching. And when your breakthrough comes, they will have to acknowledge that it must have been God! So you may be locked in prison; give God praise. Rehearse the promises of God God in praise and worship. II Corinthians 1:20 reminds us: *"For all the promises of God in Him are yea, and in Him Amen, unto the glory of God by us."* So remember you are never forgotten. Hallelujah!

You must believe God. You must take Him at His Word. Did God ever do anything for you? Has He given you your hearts desire at any time? Are your needs met? I encourage you to go back to the beginning. When you stand up, you should have some history to talk about. Think about what He did for you in your Genesis [beginning]? He made you in His own image and likeness; then blew breath into your body and you became a living soul. Amen.

Exodus: He brought you out by His Outstretched Arm, Strong Power and Mighty Arm, with riches and great wealth in good health. Think about your history. Think on how God brought your Family out. Pause and reflect on all He has done for you. Give God Praise and Glory in the Name of Jesus. Amen. Amen.

"The eyes of your understanding being enlightened; that ye may know what is the hope of His calling, and what the riches of the glory of His inheritance in the saints," (Ephesians 1:18)

Watch Fanaticism

Chapter 16

God has no limits or boundaries. Satan has limitations. He is a created being. I encourage you to get to know the Creator. When satan bothers you, seek the face of God. Continue seeking God until He intervenes. Satan cannot read your mind. Recognize negative thoughts and cast them down. The Bible says: *"Resist the devil and he will flee from you."* Know who you are in Christ Jesus.

Gullible Christians believe almost anything. They tend to believe every preacher they hear. These precious saints are easy to fleece, because they are so trusting. They look everywhere for services to attend. They possess Bibles, yet they are always in search of a Word from the LORD. Words are spoken to them such as: *"God told me to tell you."* These can be dangerous words. Satan comes as an angel of light. God can speak to us through signs and wonders. He may speak through dreams, visions and even quietness. Nonetheless, it is wise to rely fully on God's Word, The Holy Bible.

"And He [God] said, Go forth, and stand upon the mount before the LORD. And, behold, the LORD passed by, and a great and strong wind rent the mountains, and brake in pieces the rocks before the LORD; but the LORD was not in the wind: and after the wind an earthquake; but the LORD was not in the earthquake: And after the earthquake a fire; but the LORD was not in the fire: and after the fire a still small voice." (I Kings 19:11-12)

"For thus saith the Lord GOD, the Holy One of Israel; In returning and rest shall ye be saved; in quietness and in confidence shall be your strength: and ye would not." (Isaiah 30:15)

Know them that labor among you. Get to understand the character of those who are in your inner and outer circle. Know your faith in Christ. You must have faith in God. Know in whom you believe. Be persuaded that

He is able to keep that which you have committed into His hands against that day.

You are the righteousness of God in Christ Jesus. Do you know who you are? God's Word, the Bible will stand the test of time. Resist the devil and he will flee. You are not wrestling against flesh and blood according to Ephesians 6:12 *"For we wrestle not against flesh and blood, but against principalities, against powers, against the rulers of the darkness of this world, against spiritual wickedness in high places."*

Reality Check

Preachers' Kids, "You are on display." Someone is always listening and watching everything we say and do. It doesn't matter where we go or what we do, someone is watching. You are constantly on display as you go about your day-to-day activities. I want you to always remember this: *You Live in A Glass House.* You might ask why? Why must I Live in A Glass House? Why am I always on public display? My life is not an open book. My Parents' lives are but not mine. I need and desire my personal privacy.

Allow me to explain something to you. The world sees our Minister Parent(s) as being nigh to God. They are seen as God's Holy mouthpieces. They are His representatives here on this earth. Hence, they are being compared to God and the things of God. Perfection and greatness are expected from them and their posterity. Did you not know that, *"You Live in A Glass House?"* Your life is always under close scrutiny in and out of Church, school, the community, and the family. Some people feel your Minister Parent(s) are [should be] perfect. You might ask why? Well, they do spend a lot of time in God's presence seeking guidance and direction? They are constantly studying His Word – right? I remember in the Bible, when people spent time with God, their lives were changed. They didn't tolerate sin and/or ungodly foolishness.

When *Living in Glass Houses,* we are always in a demo showcase. More is expected of us because we live under the same roof as the Minister. We shouldn't desire to engage in anything, except things of Ministry: Godliness and Holiness. If it is not Scriptural-based, we should avoid it at any cost. That tends to be the attitude of the Parents of the non-Preacher

Kids. It is scandalous for us to desire participation in sports, drama or anything not Bible-based. Preachers' Kids should know better, than to even try worldly stuff, is common thought. They shouldn't disrespect their Parents like that. The question is: like what?

Everything we wear, do and say is compared to spiritual things. The fact that we are the Offspring of The Reverend Clergy sets us apart as super-spiritual. We automatically are thought to have little halos on our heads. Big brother and/or sister are always watching to see if our halos are lopsided or not. We are held up as models for their Children. Scripture says in II Corinthians 10:12: *"For we dare not make ourselves of the number, or compare ourselves with some that commend themselves: but they measuring themselves by themselves, and comparing themselves among themselves, are not wise."* The question on the floor is: "Why are you comparing?"

PKs, you are *Living in Glass Houses*. I encourage you to develop a genuine personal, trusting relationship with the Lord of Lords and King of Kings – Jesus Christ. Allow Him to heal you from the inside out, and the outside in. Come out of your secret shell. Attempting to retreat is not the answer. You are still on display. Why? The best way to handle any situation is to face it. We are Preacher's Kids! Our Parents are not perfect and neither are we. In this life, we strive towards perfection. We have been forgiven by God, our Father. His Son, Jesus Christ died to redeem us and rose to justify us, over 2000 years ago. Right now, He is sitting at the Right Hand of God making intercession for us. Aren't you glad about it?

As quite as it is kept, Preachers' Kids are not the only people *Living in Glass Houses*. Celebrities, Politicians, Athletes, Royalty and others in the public eye, also Live in Glass Houses. Their lives are also in the spotlight. We can close the doors, pull down the shades and keep the Paparazzi out. Although, we are not followed around with cameras, and other technologies, we are still under scrutiny Nonetheless, we can go to school, shopping, work and our places of worship with few problems. Many Celebrities, Royalty, Politicians, etc. may have people following them daily. That is not happening to most of us. Think about it. When you think your situation is bad, there is someone worst off than you. Remember, we are all

"*Living in Glass Houses."* Nevertheless, thank God, we are free to worship. So breathe a sigh of relief.

There is greatness in you. Let God develop the gifts that is in you. There is Ministry in you. You have excellent communication skills, leadership skills, musical skills, acts of kindness, and/or acting abilities. As Children, the entire community raised us. If you were doing something wrong, an adult would correct you before you went home. When you arrived home, your Parents followed through on the discipline. So you can see, we have always lived in *Glass Houses*. It was for our good, not detriment. Thus, we try to get over it. Some may break the law and when they come back looking for Mercy and Grace through Faith, it is always there for them. Amen.

Accept the fact that you are favored to be born to Parents who are members of The Reverend Clergy. It cannot be changed no matter how hard you wish it wasn't so. The same thing is true of your DNA. You can't change your biological Parents. Your life will be so much easier when you accept this fact. Ask God to "Order Your Steps in His Word." Accept God's guidance in every facet of your life. Trust God. He didn't make a mistake. He wasn't trying to be funny when He called your Parents into the Service of Ministry.

In Biblical days, nearly all the members of the Tribe of Levi were Priests. That tribe was set aside to meet the needs in/of the Synagogue. Some were Priests, some singers, some musicians, some were the makers of the priestly garments; some were builders; some cleaned the Synagogue, some were chefs. Some of them furnished the Synagogue. Whatever the need was in the Synagogue, a member of the Tribe of Levi was assigned to that Ministerial service or task. As a result, this was the only Tribe not given their own land grant when the Children of Israel entered the Promised Land. They received a portion of the offerings brought into the Temple. Due to their obedience to God, their needs were met.

It was in the Mind of God for you to be a child of The Reverend Clergy. Be proud of your Family. Your Parents could have been abusers, alcoholics, murderers, panderer, prostitutes, substance abusers, and the like. What would you have said about it? How would you feel if that was the case?

Would you be pleased with their lifestyles? Do you think God would be Glorified?

I know of a situation where a couple had several children. Both of the Parents had good jobs. Every weekend they got drunk – so drunk, they would often fall down in the street. Their children loved and cared for them so much, that when they were late getting home; they would go out looking for them. When found, they would pick them up out of the streets and take them home. This scenario played and replayed almost every weekend. At times, their Mom's body would be exposed. Ensuring she was okay, her cloths would be made proper, before taken home. Both Parents were always treated with loving kindness by their Children.

In spite of early difficulties, today, many of those Children are in Ministry. They are very fruitful in their choice of a vocation in God's service. And, they did not have any misbegotten Children, to my knowledge. Some of their Parents may have been alcoholics, nevertheless, they learned to respect their Parents and persevere through it all. I have never heard a word of complaint from any of them. They held their heads high and became victors not victims. To God Be the Glory!!

This would have been too much for me to handle, but they did. What about you? Could you take it? Would you have fallen apart? Should you have issues that your Parent(s) is a Preacher. Per-suppose, it was the other way around . . . they were trouble-makers. What would you have done?

You might say, "Well, I will never know." I am sure you are glad about it. Take off your mask. First: *"To thine own self be true."* God has a plan for you and yours. He wants what is best for you. He will not do anything to harm you. There are many good and precious promises that have been given to us by God from Genesis to Revelations. Read and meditate on them. Apply them to your daily lives. Get rid of the attitude. Stop the victim mentality. Realize you were born from the best of the best. Psalm 139 tells us plainly that God knows us. We were made and fashioned in the image and likeness of God, our Father. Verse 14 declares: *"I will praise thee; for I am fearfully and wonderfully made: marvellous are Thy works; and that my soul knoweth right well."*

Pastors and Spiritual Leaders, take inventory of God's way of doing things. Do not just hold Church as usual. Jesus says in Matthew 6:33: *"But seek ye first the kingdom of God, and His righteousness; and all these things shall be added unto you."* Put the Word of God first in your life. Seek His Will with your whole heart. Develop a personal relationship with God. He loves you so much. He wants to teach you how to love Him and others. Love is a matter of the heart. Learn to love yourself, and others. In return, you will be able to receive love – God's perfect love.

Your own Children are calling you hypocrites, liars and phonies because you talk love. When others are present, you demonstrate love to strangers in the street. Yet, you do not always demonstrate love in your own homes to your families. The question on the floor is: How do you justify being kind to others which ignoring your families at home?

Love is what you do *not* what you say. My Godfather always said, *"What you do speak so loud I do not hear what you say."* Your speech betrays you. I encourage you to take inventory. Take off the mask. First: *"To your own self be true."* You must be true to you, before; you can be true to me or anyone else. Bishops, Pastors, Priests, Rabbis, Elders, Missionaries, Deacons and all members of The Reverend Clergy; your Children and Family members are crying out for your love and attention. They are desirous of spending quality time with you – their Parent(s).

Dad, endeavor to spend some quality time with your daughter. Listen to her. Take her out on dates at least once a month. Show her how a man should treat a Lady. Once in a while, it is alright to cater to her. You should open doors for your daughter when she is going into and out of buildings, cars, etc. Always show her how valuable she is to you. Help her to realize her self worth. Encourage your daughter to always be a Lady above reproach, inside and outside of the home. Celebrate her, not tolerate her.

In all things, Dad, as much as possible, be an example, for your Sons and Daughters. Show them how a Husband/Father should love and care for his Family [Wife and Children.] Have Family time with them at least once a week. Include your Family in some of your devotion times. Have fun times with your Family. You must never have more time for outsiders, than you have for your Wife and Children. Try to reserve some time for them. Always putting others first, can cause a lot of unnecessary grief for you, your Wife and Children.

Many times, Dad, you expect your Family to understand why you are not spending quality time with them. Yet, they do not always realize the required allegiance. All they know is that my Dad is more concerned about making sure others are cared for, but gives little or no concern for us. Children are not just Children. They are your offspring, your seed, your posterity. They need you to show them that you care. It would not bother them that you are helping others, if your service others, did not interfere with their lives.

If you do this, it will result in a lot less pain and suffering for your Family, possibly the community and yourself. Give your children some degree of normalcy as they live their lives. Your ministerial duties are the same as a full-time job. Do not let it consume who you are. Remember: You are a man first with a Family. You should attend their recitals, ball games and other extra curriculum activities. Take them to amusement parks, the zoo, the beach, the theater, and the like. Go on vacation with your family. Do not get too busy to play with them.

Example

One day, Michael, one of my nephews was watching a football game. His son, little Michael came into the room. He asked his Dad to come outside and play with him. His Dad responded in this manner. "I am watching the game." Little Mike's response to his Dad was "What is more important to you, Dad, the game or me?" His Dad didn't have to think twice about it. The words of his son cut deeply into his heart. The television went off and outside he went to spend quality time with his son.

Tell me. What would you have done? Gods says in Psalm 127:3-5: *"Lo, children are an heritage of the LORD: and the fruit of the womb is His reward. As arrows are in the hand of a mighty man; so are children of the youth. Happy is the man that hath his quiver full of them: they shall not be ashamed, but they shall speak with the enemies in the gate."* Remember, your children did not ask to be born. You are responsible for their welfare.

Give them the love they desire, need and deserve. The return on your investment of love will be immeasurable.

Bishop, Pastor, Rabbi, Priest, Evangelist, Missionary, Deacon and other members of The Reverend Clergy: As the first family, you are role models to other families in the Houses of Worship and in the community. You are expected to be examples in so many things. You are usually the first to arrive to the Church and the last to leave. You should be a reflection of Godliness to the world; teaching and showing others what to do. There are many lonely times, when Parents are not at home with their children. In spite of that, the Cleric vocation and calling requires much attention and care to everyone; especially Family. There will be countless sweet times to cherish and enjoy at home, when the Family is together. God sees us through all our challenges and dilemmas. Scripture says in I Peter 5:7: *"Casting all your care upon him; for he careth for you."* God is good. He loves and cares for all of us. As His Stewards and Ambassadors, we must live by faith, and trust Him to never leave us nor forsake us. As His beloved children, He will enable us to enjoy precious moments with our families, as well as those we are called to serve. Amen.

You Are In Need of A Healing

Chapter 17

The name Preachers' Kids, (PK) is used to refer to Children of The Reverend Clergy, also known as: Bishop, Pastor, Priest, Rabbi, Evangelist, Missionary, Deacon and other Clerics. It is mainly used to describe the offspring of The Reverend Clergy.

We are the posterity of The Reverend Clergy. Hence, we are held to a higher standard and often subjected to greater scrutiny than other children. People around them, including their parents, often set higher moral and behavioral standards for these children. Due to the greater visibility of these children, their mistakes are often magnified and given extra attention. We are often treated differently from others. There are different sets of rules for The Preachers' Kids vs. other Children. Sometimes, this causes negative and disruptive behaviors to surface. We are often stereotyped as *holier-than-thou. We think we are better than others.* Preachers' Kids are accused of always preaching to any and every one they encounter. We rebel when we are constantly picked upon by Church folk and people in the community. Sometimes, we may deny our Parents or just do wrong behind their backs.

How does the posterity of The Reverend Clergy or Preachers' Kids withstand the pressure from congregational expectations? And how does a member of The Reverend Clergy protect his or her family? You can't keep individuals from peering in, but you can keep them from destroying your children lives. Protect your children from malicious nonsense. Protect them from the so-called do-gooders. My parents did everything imaginable to help their children to live as unto the Lord, while *"Living in A Glass House."* *They did immeasurable things to help us grow as wholesome individuals. I thank God for both Mom and Dad. My siblings and I are blessed to have had them as our parents. O' how we love and appreciate them for their love, training and discipline. They have now transitioned into their new home with the Lord.*

We had family prayer at least once per week with my Dad leading the prayer. He would pray for our well being, our protection, our prosperity, as well as, our personal relationships with Jesus Christ, God's Son. We would all kneel and pray individually for a while. After which, Dad would lead us into corporate prayer. After which, Mom would lead us into a song. Dad and Mom prayed fervently for us during their individual prayer time. *"The effectual fervent prayer of a righteous man availeth much." (James 5:16b)* They didn't know what was going on inside of us. However, they had the presence of mind to have family meetings with us so we could discuss what was happening in our lives. In retrospect, I know it was the Lord ordering their steps. They put their trust in God to take care of us at all times. They knew we had need of the Holy Spirit to sustain, guide and protect us.

During our family time, Dad would re-iterate that we should never let anyone put us down because of what we do or do not have, the color of our skin, our size or whatever. We are as good as or better than anyone walking on two feet. Those statements are as much a part of me today as they were when I was a child. Dad instilled in his children the assurance needed to help us live from day to day. Mom taught Community Bible Study in our living room. Mom and Dad taught us to trust God with our whole hearts. Simply, take God at His Word, and in all things, put our confidence in Him.

Dad gave us the freedom to be children. He let us play sports, go to the movies with our friends and family, laugh and have fun. We were given limited freedom. I overheard some ladies from the Church tell Dad, "Mom was going to make him go to hell, because we had those freedoms." But he was not moved by their remarks. He did not let them rule his home. Dad and Mom wanted us to be happy, well-rounded individuals. I thank God for giving us to them and them to us.

Man is born in sin and shapened in iniquity as everyone born into this world. As long as we live in these houses of clay, we are subject to sin. This flesh we are living in is an enemy of God. Dad stressed the importance of letting go and letting God have His way in our lives. He stressed the importance of transparency. We must tell him the truth. If he ever caught us in an untruth; it meant discipline for us. What did that mean? We would be chastised with love and self-control. When we failed at something, Dad and Mom were there to encourage us to try again. They did not hesitate to tell us how much they loved us and to show their love to each other in front of us. We did need to know that, in our failure, Dad and Mom loved and accepted us as we were; so does God our heavenly Father.

Dad always tried to protect us from the outside world. He was a very wise man. We knew he loved us and cared more deeply about us than the external appearance of his earthly ministry. Our parents never sent us on guilt trips. Dad was not bound by what people thought. He loved us and taught us Biblical principles.

Dad would assert his authority when Church members overstepped their boundaries where his family was concerned. He stood up in a Church meeting and made some statements about his family advising them to back off. Mom was his Spouse. We were his children. My Dad quickly stepped in to protect his family. He didn't show favoritism toward his Kids in the Church, but he was willing to defend us when necessary. Before we would go to Church, Dad told us that we should not play with God. It didn't matter what the other children did. We should not follow suit. If we did, Dad would give us a good licking when we went home. God is not a plaything. Do not play with God. Be real for God not a fake. We obeyed Dad because we knew he had our best interest at heart and it helped that we did not want a licking. Dad and Mom enforced the boundary between our family and our Church members. Their loving kindness and decisive action allowed us to follow our goals.

Reverend Clergy, allow your children to explore what God has put in their hearts. My Parents were Spiritual Leaders. An entire Church, the community, and, the WJAY 1280 AM Radio listening audience, in South Carolina, looked to them for guidance. I was keenly aware of their status in the community, and to be honest, I didn't want to share them in the beginning with outsiders. Dad explained that the call of God on his life did not mean that he would not be there for us. I could go to my Dad at any time, for anything: big or small.

Members of The Reverend Clergy have asked me, "How did you make it? How can I help my Kids make it?" Ultimately, it's all about the Grace of God, but I am convinced that my Parents' application of the Word of God is why we are where we are today. I thank God for all He has done for us. Preachers' Kids, although you may be hurting, don't give up. God is real! Negative feelings maybe churning on the inside of you. I too, have experienced pain. I use to allow negative feelings to overwhelm me due to Church people making digs at me. One day I came to grips with the fact, that I Am A King's Kid. There is nothing anyone can say that can change that fact. I do not have to feed into their issues. I know who I am in Christ Jesus. The scripture says: "For we are his workmanship, created in Christ Jesus unto good works, which God hath before ordained that we should walk in them." (Ephesians 2:10)

The Life of Preachers' Kids

Chapter 18

I want you to think of what it is like being a PK or Preachers' Kid? Did you at any time consider the other kids in the Church and or Synagogue who are not PKs? It seems to be okay for the Children of the Laity to behave a certain way. However, if their Parent(s) are members of The Reverend Clergy, they are looked upon as horrible people. How many times has a Preachers' Kid been told "You can't do this or that because people won't like it?" They won't understand.

How many Children of The Reverend Clergy missed out on a normal childhood? Many Parents would not let their Children experience life, because people might talk? You couldn't go to the movies. It just didn't look right. If people see you at the movies and/or at a sporting event; they may not attend our Church. How many Preachers' daughters were made to wear dresses because Preachers' daughters do not, and/or should not dress like the world? How is wearing something other than a dress looking or dressing like the world?

Example

My Sisters and I had to wear dresses all of the time. When it was extremely cold, my Mom would put pants on us under our dresses. We had to take the pants off when we arrived at school. The Church Women did not like it at all. My Parents were ridiculed because of it; they condemned my Dad to hell. During the summer, we would go to the beach. When we went to the beach, my sisters and I wore denim skirts and T-shirts. However, my Brothers could wear shorts but the girls, could not. Imagine the weight of denim during the 60's. When the denim was wet, it was very heavy as we walked down the beach. It felt like we were carrying a sack of potatoes. We were wearing wet T-shirts on the beach before they were popular. Today, I do not enjoy going to the beach, although I can wear what I choose. We always had to set examples for every one in the community including the Church.

Preachers' Kids weren't allowed to fall asleep in a Church service. It didn't matter that all the other children were asleep. Question? Were not they also supposed to reverence God? If we went to sleep in Church, we were awakened immediately. Other children could lie out on the benches and their parents would not wake them. It was okay. I call that a double standard.

Many PKs were not allowed to participate in sports at school. Dad and Mom did allow us to play sports but many of the Preachers Kids I have met later in life could not. Their parents were doing God's work, and their after-school sport activity would interfere with the Ministry. God might get angry if they didn't have an evening service, but they went to a ball game. Some might say it is sacrilegious. They are not raising their Children in the fear of God. Preachers' Kids must always be in Church, but their children could stay home and go to ball games.

It wasn't always easy being a Preachers' Kid. Ofttimes, we are ignored because our Parents are ministering to other people. When Parents have taken care of Ministerial responsibilities, they were too tired to give their Children what they needed. As we grew into adulthood, we became "miniature" Bishops, Pastors, Preachers, Evangelists, Rabbis, Priests, Missionaries, Deacons, etc. Yet, we are different. This lesson should be learned early in life. Many times during Sunday School Class, and/or Vacation Bible School; where Mom [the Preachers' Wife] is teaching. When the supplies are short, the Preachers' Kids may not get their necessary supplies. It was imperative that the others were served first. It is okay if you do not get one. You must tough it up and understand. Dear Parents, we have feelings, too. We are Children also . . . your Children. We want to feel special to you; to God, to Jesus and the Holy Spirit. It does not seem fair to us. We are the ones that do not get the crafts, the trinkets and novelties while attending Vacation Bible School (VBS). We are often told that we should understand that our Parents must reach others for Christ. Yes, but Parents, what about us. We, too, have souls to be saved. We would like to be special to you. When our feelings get hurt, we feel rejected.

Preachers, don't try to save the world while your Wife and Children are often discouraged.

Our Parents are Ministers and for some reason the community expects us to be replicas of them. That means, we would skip our childhood. If the Worship Leader doesn't come to Church, we are to fill in. We are acting Ushers; Choir members; Offering collectors; Trustees and Deacons, until a Member comes to Church. For Preachers' Kid life can be lonely. We are not invited to parties, or social occasions, nor can we get together outside of Church.

Parents hosting the get-together don't want us to come to their homes; peradventure we tell the Minister Parent(s) what happens. The other children are not permitted to tell us what happened at the parties, either. This is the scenario: the children that attended the party are talking about it among themselves. You can hear them laughing and talking. You walk up and ask why they are laughing. Their reply is nothing. They look at each other and snicker. You feel worst than before you asked them. You feel shunned and ostracized. Preacher's Kids do not have a lot of space.

Although these things are happening to us, we are expected to continue in leadership roles at Church, without fail. They tell us this: Remember people are watching you. The children are often watched to ascertain how the family is living at home. Well-behaved, happy Kids signify a good Christian home. If you are misbehaving, and not actively involved in your Parents' Ministry, something must wrong with them [your Parents]. They would throw out tit-bits from Scripture such as I Timothy 3:5: *"(For if a man know not how to rule his own house, how shall he take care of the church of God?)"* We are expected to be walking Bibles. We are thought to be super-spiritual and never rebellious. If we do anything that they feel we should not do, we are considered *the worst kind.*

What would make us rebel against our parents? Do you think we awakened one day and decided I am going to rebel? Is it something we planned for a while? Were we forced into it? Is it a cry for help and/or attention from our parents? What is it?

Consider this? It may be the only time we get attention from our parents. When we are being reprimanded for something we were accused of, our parents listened. Perhaps, at times, punishment filled the need to be recognized. As a result, we are seen as separate persons, apart from our parents. We are tired of trying to be what others want us to be. We want to be different. We desire to be ourselves, not an image of our Parents.

Preachers' Kids sometimes get fed up, rebel and turn away from the Church as the prodigal son when he left home. But most of the time we do not go far. We realize there is nothing in the world but destruction. We go to these parties and the heathens at the party look at us and say: *"What are you doing here? You know you do not belong here."* Heathens know we do not belong, even when we are rebelling and trying to fit in. After a while, we get sick and tired of being sick and tired and turn back to God, and the things of God. He did not leave us. We left Him. It isn't long before we realize, no matter how far we go; God is still watching over us. If we get off track, experiment with things of the world; we have been grounded on Rock. We should repent and turn back to God, just as the Lost [Prodigal] Son returned to his Father. (See Luke 15:11-24)

Example

One day, a Preachers' Kid was sitting outside of the Church in a parked car, talking with her cousin. She was subsequently accused of smoking, by a Church member. This individual, hurriedly, told her Pastor Dad. She was chastised by her parents. Soon after, it was discovered that the incident was not true. Some PKs may do drugs: legal and/or illegal; others get involved in premarital sex and/or whatever. Afterward, we are considered backsliders. It is a known Biblical saying: "God is married to the backslider." God says in Jeremiah 3:14: *"Turn, O backsliding children, saith the LORD; for I am married unto you:"* Again God says in Jeremiah 3:22: *"Return, ye backsliding children, and I will heal your backslidings."* We are expected to come to ourselves. We are then encouraged to repent and return to God. Remorse and repentance is all that is required. God is perceived as a loving Father, waiting for His children with open arms.

Don't be so hard on a Preachers' Kid, just because Dad is a member of The Reverend Clergy. Just because the family is in Ministry doesn't make them any less of a Kid. So don't be so hard on PKs. Remember, oftentimes, Preachers' Kids have never had a childhood. The Cleric has been too busy dealing with needs of Parishioners, to spend as much time, with his family, as he would have liked. Why don't you make a special effort to pray for the Preacher, the Spouse and the Kids? Perhaps, you can pitch in, by offering to spend time with them. After all, their parents do so much for you and the community.

How do I know these feelings and such? That's easy; I'm a Preacher's Kid. If you are one also, you might want to celebrate the life you were given. Let's stop bellyaching and embrace the family business. It is not always the pulpit. It is a worldwide, day by day Ministry. The family business is in need of behind the scenes, specialty people, such as information technology and professional support. Everyone is not called to the Frontline. We need all you, from across America, and around the world to strengthen the PK Alliance. Let's continue to grow from *"strength to strength."* (See Psalm 84:7)

The Great Commission: *"And He [Jesus] said unto them, Go ye into all the world, and preach the gospel to every creature."*
(Mark 16:15)

We must allow God to rise up in us, through us and by us. Preachers' Kids, I know you are hurting. At times, there are countless negative feelings, churning on the inside of us. I, also, feel the pain of caring for others. Pain hurts no matter who is suffering. "Rise Up O' God, hear the voice of Preachers' Kids, show Yourself strong on our behalf." Thank You LORD for calling our Parents and families. We are grateful to You for choosing us as PKs.

Rev. Dr. Arnetha Bowens

Scriptures to Encourage

"And the afflicted people Thou wilt save: but Thine eyes are upon the haughty, that Thou mayest bring them down."
(II Samuel 22:28)

"Thou shalt hide them in the secret of Thy presence from the pride of man: Thou shalt keep them secretly in a pavilion from the strife of tongues."
(Psalm 31:20)

"For the sin of their mouth and the words of their lips let them even be taken in their pride: and for cursing and lying which they speak."
(Psalm 59:12)

"Surely men of low degree are vanity, and men of high degree are a lie: to be laid in the balance, they are altogether lighter than vanity." (Psalm 62:9)

"Whoso privily slandereth his neighbour, him will I cut off: him that hath an high look and a proud heart will not I suffer."
(Psalm 101:5)

"LORD, my heart is not haughty, nor mine eyes lofty: neither do I exercise myself in great matters, or in things too high for me."
(Psalm 131:1)

"Though the LORD be high, yet hath He respect unto the lowly: but the proud He knoweth afar off." (Psalm 138:6)

"The fear of the LORD is to hate evil: pride, and arrogancy, and the evil way, and the froward mouth, do I hate."
(Proverbs 8:13)

"When pride cometh, then cometh shame: but with the lowly is wisdom."
(Proverbs 11:2)

Scriptures to Encourage
(continued)

"Pride goeth before destruction, and an haughty spirit before a fall." (Proverbs 16:18)

"Better it is to be of an humble spirit with the lowly, than to divide the spoil with the proud." (Proverbs 16:19)

"Before destruction the heart of man is haughty; and before honour is humility." (Proverbs 18:12)

"Most men will proclaim every one his own goodness: but a faithful man who can find?" (Proverbs 20:6)

"Proud and haughty scorner is his name, who dealeth in proud wrath." (Proverbs 21:24)

"There is a generation that are pure in their own eyes, and yet is not washed from their filthiness." (Proverbs 30:12)

"Extol not thyself in the counsel of thine own heart; that thy soul be not torn in pieces as a bull [straying alone]."
(Ecclesiastes 6:2)

"Better is the end of a thing than the beginning thereof: and the patient in spirit is better than the proud in spirit."
(Ecclesiastes 7:8)

"The Lord only is righteous, and there is none other but He,"
(Ecclesiastics 18:2)

"He that findeth his life shall lose it: and he that loseth his life for My sake shall find it." (Matthew 10:39)

Scriptures to Encourage
(continued)

"But we are all as an unclean thing, and all our righteousnesses are as filthy rags; and we all do fade as a leaf; and our iniquities, like the wind, have taken us away." (Isaiah 64:6)

"But go ye and learn what that meaneth, I WILL HAVE MERCY, AND NOT SACRIFICE: for I am not come to call the righteous, but sinners to repentance." (Matthew 9:13)

-Prayer-

Father in Jesus Name,

I confess it is not always easy to obey our Parents. Sometimes, I think they are wrong. I can only obey them with Your help. Help me. I desire to obey Your Word and be in compliance with Your Will. I am looking unto You, Jesus, the Author and Finisher of my faith. Give me all that I have need of, to be who You want me to be.

Father, I ask this in Jesus Name. Amen.

I trust in You, LORD with my whole heart. I will not lean unto my own understanding. Help me to be a blessing on a daily basis. I desire Your perfect will to be done in my life. I love you LORD. Thank You LORD for calling me, and making me according to Your own good pleasure. Use me for Your glory. In Jesus Name. Amen. Amen.

Children of The Reverend Clergy

Chapter 19

Let Me Encourage You With These Words . . .

God loves you. He has chosen you for a time and a purpose to bring honor to Him. God has His hands on our lives. We were covered by God before we were born. You and your family have been objects of satanic attack. He is trying to destroy you by using people in your inner circle: family, friends, classmates, neighbors, colleagues, teachers, Church members, as well as those in authority.

These people have allowed the enemy to use their mouths to anesthetize you. Their words were poisonous as they spewed out of their mouths. James 3:5-10 tells us: *"Even so the tongue is a little member, and boasteth great things. Behold, how great a matter a little fire kindleth! And the tongue is a fire, a world of iniquity: so is the tongue among our members, that it defileth the whole body, and setteth on fire the course of nature; and it is set on fire of hell. For every kind of beasts, and of birds, and of serpents, and of things in the sea, is tamed, and hath been tamed of mankind: But the tongue can no man tame; it is an unruly evil, full of deadly poison. Therewith bless we God, even the Father; and therewith curse we men, which are made after the similitude of God. Out of the same mouth proceedeth blessing and cursing. My brethren, these things ought not so to be."* Some of these people profess to love you, but their words and deeds say something totally different.

You now have low self-esteem. You feel inadequate, unsure of yourself, less than a man, less than a woman. You have forgotten that you are made in the image and likeness of God our Father. In the Book of the beginnings, Genesis, we find this truth. God molded man into His image blew the breath of life into him and man became a living soul. Didn't you know that

God did not make a mistake when He formed you? God knows your end from your beginning. He is acquainted with all your ways.

God the Father, God the Son, God the Holy Spirit, three in one, is always looking out for you. He wants me to remind you of your importance to Him. You are the 'Apple of His eye'. He is not trying to take any thing away from you. He wants to give you all you need and so much more. Although, Anesthetizes may have told you that you were a mistake, a nothing. You will never be nothing, but the devil is a liar and the father of lies. God is the giver and sustainer of life. You are not a surprise to Him. If the truth be told, you are not a surprise to your Parents. They knew what it would take to make a baby before you were conceived. Do not get caught up in negative rhetoric about your conception. You are here by the Grace of God. He is keeping you on a daily basis from dangers seen and unseen, even in your foolishness. Praise God!

God is keeping you in the good and bad times. You may have walked away from God and the things of God, but He is still looking out for you. He is opening doors that have been closed in your face. Didn't you know that you are the righteousness of God in Christ Jesus? Children of The Reverend Clergy, come home today. Reclaim your inheritance. Take back what the devil stole from you.

A few years ago, while I was visiting South Carolina, I saw a former classmate of one of my sisters. He said to me, *You were voted least likely to succeed.* He was not in my class. He tried to date me when we were younger. Now this drunkard is standing before me with nonsense. My response was: *"Maybe that was your vote, but God. You may have counted me out, but God. I am so glad you are not in control of my destiny."* His reply, *"I can see that I was wrong."* I began to share with him the Good News about Jesus. Of course, he did not want to hear it, so he left hurriedly.

Opines from An Anesthetizer

Arnetha, girl, it is so good to see you. You all are doing a good job, helping your Mother. Mother Bowens wears very nice clothes. Every one can see how well you all take care of her. I stood there smiling, yet letting her know that Mother Bowens is also my friend. She took care of us along with Dad, so it is our time to take care of her. Here is the clincher: *"You sure look good, but you are so fat."* My response was: *"We can't all be small like*

Mom. Some of us had to take after my Dad." What happened? She repeated what she had said initially about my size. The third time she said it was too much for me to handle.

I was trying to be nice and remind her of this truth that my Dad, Bishop Bowens, was a large man. But it was not working, so I decided to nip this in the bud. I thought about the scripture that says, *"Agree with thine adversary quickly whilst you are in the way with him."* My next words were: *I might be fat, but . . .* the but negated everything I said first. I canceled satan's plots and plans for me. I pulled down his strongholds. *To God Be the Glory!* My entire sentence was: *I might be fat, but I am so fine.* Her response: *"Girl you are something else."* I said: "Yes, Maam. I am my Mom and Dad's daughter." Her response, *"I better let you go, Mother Bowens is probably waiting for you."* I hugged her, and off I went. This happened years ago. From that time to this, she has never mentioned another word to me about my size. When I go home, I see her occasionally, but my size has not come up any more.

While living in Pennsylvania, a so-called friend came to visit. After we embraced she said, "You are always changing your hair. One day it is short; one day it is long. I do not know what to expect from you from day to day. Do you push a button on your back like they do on doll babies to make their hair long or short?" It was time to nip this foolishness in the bud. I laughed and said: *"Variety is the spice of life. I am so glad with the hair that is on my head. I can do with it as I please. I have choices."* It was none of her business what I did with the hair on my head. As I write this chapter, I am reminded of a statement my Aunt Dollie Mae used to say, *"Give me back my business."* Aren't you tired of folk minding your business? You can't stop them from talking but you can get them out of your business.

When I turned fifty plus, someone called to wish me a Happy Birthday. Their question, *"Did you ever think you would turn fifty plus? What do you mean? Yes. I thought I would turn this age. As a matter of fact, I expect to live until I am (120) one hundred twenty. Longevity runs in my family."* (See Genesis 6:3) She shut her mouth. I am tired of the devil. How about you? If you are not paying close attention, the adversary will have you agreeing with nonsense, putting natural laws into motion. These laws are put into motion by the seeds that you sow out of your mouths. Proverbs 18:21a reveals that: *"Death and life are in the power of the tongue:"* Remember: watch your tongue. It is not what I say about you, it is what you say about you.

Children of The Reverend Clergy (CoTRC) – First: "To thine own self be true." It is time to take off the mask. Be real with yourself. Take responsibility for your own position in this life. Forgive the offenders. Return to God. Let Him heal your wounds. He is a healer of the broken heart. Let Him heal you from the inside out. Cast all of your cares upon the Lord. Simply, cry out to God. Tell Him all about your hurts, pains, disappointments and rejections. Take it all to the Cross where Jesus hung, bled and died for you. Ask God to forgive you, and help your unforgiveness.

From This Day Forth

Chapter 20

No More Excuses

No more excuses. No more excuses. No more excuses. It is time to come out of Lodebar where you have been hiding. Come and take your rightful place at the King's table. You have been in Lodebar far too long. The feast has been prepared. The table has been set. God has prepared a table before you in the presence of your enemies. It is time to come and dine. Read Genesis, chapter 9. It tells a story of David looking for someone in Saul's family that he could show kindness.

Mephibosheth, Jonathan's son, was hiding in Lodebar. His nurse hid him because she was afraid that he would be killed. David sent for him and restored him to Royalty. CoTRC, Lodebar is not the place for you. You were chosen by God to be strong and do exploits. All the plots and plans of the devil have been done away. God sent His only Begotten Son – Jesus to pay the debt in full. When Jesus said, *It is finished,* while hanging on the Cross, it was indeed finished!! The price to redeem mankind back to God has been paid in full. All of your needs have been met. The curse has been reversed. Your enemy has been defeated. Every stronghold has been broken off of your life. Every generational curse canceled. The sacrifice has been received as a sweet smell in the nostrils of Almighty God. Jesus broke the curse off of our lives. The curse of poverty, lack, sickness, disease and infirmities has been broken – once and for all. When Jesus said, *It is finished.* That means, everything He came into the earth to accomplish was complete.

When people try to speak negative words over your life, do not receive them. You are as good as or better than anyone walking on two feet, my Dad, Bishop Bowens always said. Never let anyone put you down because of anything. So stop the negativity and simply put your trust in God. We can always rely upon His Word. When we pray, we are talking to God in the Name of Jesus; when we study God's Word, He is answering us, and directing our paths in righteousness. When faced with adversity of any kind, my Aunt Bernice, *"Bless her Memory,"* would always say: *"None of these things shall move me. I will not allow this, or any other nonsense to reside in my spirit."* Throughout her life, she always depended upon the steadfast Word of the Living God.

Thus, no problem can break you unless you let it. You have to sign for it. Meaning – If you do not make the issues yours, they will not affect you. May the blessing of the Lord that make rich and add no sorrow continue to be with you and yours today, tomorrow, this week, this month, this year and the rest of your lives. Take God at His word. He watches over His Word to perform it.

"Behold, the days come, saith the LORD, that the plowman shall overtake the reaper, and the treader of grapes him that soweth seed; and the mountains shall drop sweet wine, and all the hills shall melt.

And I will bring again the captivity of My people of Israel, and they shall build the waste cities, and inhabit them; and they shall plant vineyards, and drink the wine thereof; they shall also make gardens, and eat the fruit of them.

And I will plant them upon their land, and they shall no more be pulled up out of their land which I have given them, saith the LORD thy God."
(Amos 9:13-15)

LORD, Your Word, says so. Amen.

Dear Friend: Look for it. It is yours. It is ours. *Hallelujah!!!*

It is my sincere prayer that this Book has made, will make and is making a positive difference in your life. I love you with the love of the Lord Jesus Christ. "Now, Go Forth in Christ Jesus and Prosper."

Enjoy,

Arnetha

Words of Encouragement: Bishop Joseph P. Bowens

Chapter 21

Change Your Thoughts

Change your thinking; change your life. Change your life; change your destiny. Your thoughts can affect your attitude; your mood, as well as your future. Thoughts can make you miserable; in turn, you make others miserable. Thoughts can make you happy; in turn, you make others happy. Philippians 4:8 tells us plainly what we should think on. *"Finally, brethren, whatsoever things are true, whatsoever things are honest, whatsoever things are just, whatsoever things are pure, whatsoever things are lovely, whatsoever things are of good report; if there be any virtue, and if there be any praise, think on these things."* Stop vacillating between two opinions. There is a battle going on for and in the minds of men, women, boys and girls.

Satan is a deceiver and a liar. He wants you to blame external forces for all of your misery when in actuality; you are the culprit. Introspection is needed on a regular basis. Think about what you are allowing to take up residency in your mind. Erase all negative mind chatter. No matter the struggle, anticipate payday which is the day when this will all be over. When sufferings are compared with payday there is no comparison. Your light afflictions are not to be compared to the Glory that shall be revealed in us. This too shall pass, sooner rather than later.

God is preparing you for your destiny. Whatever you are growing through at this time is called development. Life spouts happen to every one of us. Renew your mind with the Word of God in accordance with Romans 12:1-2, and prosper. Explore ways to take yourself away from your situation and your troubles. Dare to dream. There is something better.

Learn from the challenges of yesterday. What you are going through is growth. Today is another day. Praise God!!

Ask the LORD to renew your mind. Let me say this again. Be not conformed to this world, but be transformed by the renewing of your mind. There is something better. You do not have to settle. Do not allow anyone to dictate to you. Believe in God and yourself. God has the last say. It doesn't matter what people say; but God. You will realize suddenly that you can lead as well as follow. Through all of your trials, test, temptation and tribulation, know God has it all under His control.

Know this: You can be in Church and out of Church at the same time. It is a mind thing. But thank God for salvation. Don't give up. Keep praying. Before long, you will see God turn it around for you. Aren't you glad the LORD gave you a chance? Aren't you glad the LORD saved you? Are you sure about your salvation? Before it is too late, will you turn your life over to Jesus? God specializes in things that seem to be impossible.

You have been hanging out in the chicken coup with chickens. Every time you try to fly, there is some negativity. Someone is telling you that it will not and/or cannot work. Stop hanging out with chickens. You are an eagle. Throw those chickens some chicken feed. You go on and soar on wings of an eagle to heights unknown.

Rise Up Father God. Hear the Voice of Your Children. Show Yourself Strong in Every Facet of Our Lives. Amen.

"Rise up, LORD, and let Thine enemies be scattered; and let them that hate Thee flee before Thee." (Numbers 10:35b)

Epilogue: Merging the Trek

Chapter 22

In Summary

We have traveled from chapter to chapter. As a result, we made our way through to the second-half of Preachers' Kids: Living in Glass Houses. Here our travels blended the two sections. The last chapter that we reviewed was chapter eleven. Passing through the middle of our book, let's turn the spotlight on Chapter 12: The Isness of God. As we press forward, let's take a little time out to think on the reality of God, our heavenly Father.

Who is God to you? He may have healed some of you. You can say: The LORD is Jehovah Rapha; my healer. I stopped by to tell you, He is better than that. Perhaps, God has delivered many of you. So you can truly say: The LORD is my deliverer. Yet, He is better than that. You may say God has performed miracles in my life. You can say without a doubt, that God is a miracle worker. I can tell you that He is more than that to His children. Take a few minutes, and let's meditate on The Isness of God. Think about it: The Isness of God . . . very revealing as to His presence and impact in our lives. Do you really know who God is? Psalm 46:10 tells us to: *"Be still, and know that I am God: I will be exalted among the heathen, I will be exalted in the earth."* So think about God's involvement in every facet of your life. The Isness of our God. Simply be still and know . . . God is God. The right now presence of God is in all that concerns us. As we reflect on the Isness of God, there is cause to stop, and give Him praise. Hallelujah! Let's give God praise for all He has done and is still doing, and/or will do in our lives. He loves us and wants what is best for us. God has shown His love to us in His Holy Word, the Bible from Genesis 1:1 through Revelations 22:21. Hallelujah. Amen. Amen.

As we perceive the "Fruit of the Spirit" as enumerated in Galatians 5:22-23, we see God's genuine dimensions of love. These attributes remind me of turning a house into a home. Love must permeate every aspect of that residence. You will be amazed as you watch a union of love transform a dwelling house into a home. *"But the fruit of the Spirit is love, joy, peace, longsuffering, gentleness, goodness, faith, Meekness, temperance: against such there is no law."* These nine Godly attributes are worthy of repetition.

- LOVE
- JOY
- PEACE
- LONGSUFFERING
- GENTLENESS
- GOODNESS
- FAITH
- MEEKNESS
- TEMPERANCE

The Scripture says: *"Against such there is no law."* Nonetheless, it is obvious that love is the key. Love is the beginning and temperance is the end. God is the source of all life. *"God is love."* The Apostle Paul says in I Corinthians 13:13: *"but the greatest of these is charity* [love]." Although, the Apostle contrasts the attributes of faith, hope and charity; yet he drew a distinction in verse eight: when he said: *"Love never fails."* Then he concludes in verse 13: *"And now abideth faith, hope, charity, these three; but the greatest of these is charity* [love]. The greatest attribute of all times is love. Love is what motivated God to send His Son, Jesus to die for our sins. Love is the power that kept our Lord and Savior, Jesus Christ on the cross in obedience to God, His Father. Love gave us another Comforter, the Holy Spirit to dwell with us and be in us. Praise God, He is leading and guiding us into all truths, right now. *"Greater love hath no man than this, that a man lay down his life for his friends.* (John 15:13) *"And we have known and believed the love that God hath to us. God is love; and he that dwelleth in love dwelleth in God, and God in him."* (I John 4:16)

As we press forth, we perused Chapter 13: The Call of God. Think about this. We are given a divine calling from Almighty God. He invites us into His Presence in answer to His call. God has called us to show the world that He lives. We are His living testimonies that God is real. He desires to show the world what He will do in our lives if we yield ourselves to His will. He wants to love mankind through you. God wants us to see Him as Papa God, Father, Dad. He desires an intimate loving relationship with us. God has a plan for our lives to show us love and not evil. Love the LORD with all your heart. Put Him first in all you do and say.

Children of those who serve; Preachers' Kid, there is a call of God on your life. God wants to use you to make a difference in this world. Your upbringing was not a surprise to God. As quiet as it is kept, His will is to be glorified in us. Will you let go and let God? Will you let Him use you for His glory? I am not saying to preach or teach. However, there is a call for you to fulfill your destiny.

The Prophet Isaiah received a divine call. See Isaiah chapter six. Verse eight says: *"Also I heard the voice of the LORD, saying, Whom shall I send, and who will go for us? Then said I, Here am I; send me."* You may not like to be center stage. Perhaps, your call is behind the scenes. All things are not out-front. Someone has to bring up the rear. We can't fulfill the front line without the other team players. Your part in the Family of God is a part of the whole. God wants His entire team. We need you and your God-given gifts, talents, abilities, expertise and skill-sets to build, grow, endure and overcome. Did you know? Do you realize? Do you understand that the thing frustrating you the most may be what you have been called to do for God? What do you go to sleep with? What do you wake up with it on a daily basis? God has deposited the answer within you. Are you using it? The Call of God is within you. As the Prophet Isaiah, will you answer The Call of God on your life?

Today, our travels have brought us to Chapter 14: The Zealous Clergy and The Spouse. While we are here, let's have a direct conversation about your family. You, your Spouse, as well as your Children represent the Ministerial Family. If today, you take off the Clergy articles of clothing, you may be told the truth. The Clergy cloth demands respect. Hence, you may not be aware that your Spouse and Children are living in neglectful pain. Even they view you as Holy. Thus, it is often difficult to discuss every day affairs with you. Your Family unit may be in jeopardy of being disassembled. A deficient environment can cause Family members to become resentful of God, Church, Synagogue, Ministry, as well as all things faith-based, and/or religious. You might question why, when you are living for God, all you know. Yet, disquiet may be happening, because your family feel alienated from you. Frequently, you may make decisions that not only affect you, but your entire Family. For example, when you quit your job, they discovered it, the same time it is announced to the Congregation that you felt led into full-time Ministry. Now that you are in full-time Ministry, they tend to be unsure of their basic human needs being met. When God calls you into the Ministry and you are married, it is not you alone in Ministry. Your decisions will affect your Spouse and Children.

When God calls you, there has to be preparation time. A charge of God on your life needs to be discussed in Family meetings. He called you because He loves you. Hence, God will never throw you to the wolves. Don't despair, nor get so busy due to your own expectations that your Family suffers. The Call of God is to you, your Spouse, and your Children. Ministry is a Family affair.

Wake up! Wake up! Wherever you are, wake up! Stop running ahead of God. Do you realize, when you are married, your actions will surpass your Family? It can some times create a domino affect. So Reverend Clergy, realize that on occasion, you may have to hit the pause button in your life. Stop being so celestial minded that you tend to do little earthly good. Do not put anything in front of the welfare and care of your Family. Your Spouse and Children need you. They desire and need to spend quality time with you. You tend to neglect yourself by neglecting your Spouse, your Children and your responsibilities to them. One solution is to have regular family meetings and devotion time with them. Tell them the things that God has spoken to your heart. Have a discussion about life in Ministry with them. Pray with them. God calls Families, not just the Leaders. You are not serving alone. Unless, Family consciousness is implemented, you will likely push your Family away from God into the hands of the adversary. You may be unaware of the potential consequences. Family breaches require love with consideration. When your Spouse and/or Children are pulling away from God; divine introspection and prayer intercession are greatly needed.

Reverend Clergy, once again, I encourage you to stop the hostilities toward your Children. Allow them to develop into well rounded boys and girls. Today, make a decision to love your family back to life. Ask God, where and how you have fallen short of His perfect will for your life? Seek Him to show you the error of your ways. Ask God to unstop your ears that you will hear the concerns of your Family. Let them know they matter to you. God promises total restoration; albeit, you must be willing to do your part.

We have now made our way to Chapter 15: Who Are These People? The question on the floor is do you know who these people are? Again, who are these people? They are Children of those who serve humanity. Their Parents and/or Guardians are helping the masses, sometimes at the expense of their Children. Many Children of The Reverend Clergy often feel neglected, excluded, ostracized, rejected, or merely shunned. Some of them are in continual inner pain. Their hearts and lives hurt. A lot of them are searching for love in all the incorrect places. The way of life some have taken is exploring evil diabolical things.

"Pain hurts, no matter who is crying." Take an optimistic staunch and endeavor to face your distress. Trust the love of God to see you through the hurting and suffering. The more you suppress agony and misery, the more difficult it is to deal with the actual pain. Thus, I speak Shalom . . . wholeness, nothing missing, nothing broken into your life. It is time to be healed. Receive your healing, in the Name of Jesus. Amen. Amen.

Studying and rehearsing God's Word will strengthen and re-affirm your faith. Let God's Word resonate in your heart, mind and spirit. Should you find yourself struggling with undue situations or relentless circumstances, wondering how God will come through for you, meditate in God's Word. Look forward through the Eyes of Faith to God's Grace and Mercy. While taking a stand, you have the testimonies of God as reference material. In your Genesis of Beginning, what has God done for you? As you go through your Exodus, see God bringing you out with His Strong Power and Out Stretched Arm. Hallelujah!! Remember how God brought you out. Always, give all the Glory to Him. He is worthy of all Praise and Honor. Amen. Praise God in advance, for hearing and answering your prayers. As you give God the Praise and Glory He deserves, Worship Him in the Beauty of Holiness. Colossians 3:16 instructs us to: *"Let the word of Christ dwell in you richly in all wisdom; teaching and admonishing one another in psalms and hymns and spiritual songs, singing with grace in your hearts to the Lord."*

Journeying onward, here we are at Chapter 16: Watch Fanaticism. Never permit yourself to become a gullible Christian. When you encounter someone who is peddling, and preaching an extreme doctrine, avoid them. Do not get caught up in religious dogma that does not acknowledge Jesus Christ, the Son of God, as Lord and Savior. Make sure that they are not advancing another Gospel, something that is not of God. Single-minded zeal can lead many astray. Watch fanaticism. Deflect people who are so heavenly minded that they appear to be no earthly good. So let's have a reality check. Preachers' Kids, know who you are in Christ Jesus. Know what it means to be an offspring of The Reverend Clergy. As their posterity, we were born to uphold the Blood Stained Banner of Christ. This is our life, this is our Ministry. *"Holding forth the word of life; that I may rejoice in the day of Christ, that I have not run in vain, neither laboured in vain."* (Philippians 2:16)

Always be vigilant. There may be people eavesdropping on your conversations. Today, living in a new found digital world, you may discover that it is difficult to maintain any degree of privacy. You are Living in Glass Houses. Your lives are always under close scrutiny in and out of Church, school, work, community, as well as your Family. Since our lives seem to be on display, we must develop a personal, trusting relationship with our LORD Jesus Christ. Let's allow Him to heal us from the inside out. Retreating inside oneself is not the answer. A good way to handle any situation is to face it with steadfast unmovable faith in Christ.

It was in the Mind of God for you to be a Child of The Reverend Clergy. people, and/or other Public Servants living in the spotlight. Your Parents were not a mistake. God chose you for them and them for you. We know that every good and perfect gift comes from God. You are one of those gifts. Explore what God has put into your heart, mind and spirit for the benefit of the Kingdom of God and all humanity.

As we navigate our path, chapter after chapter, we have arrived at Chapter 17: You Are In Need of A Healing. As Preachers' Kids: Living in Glass Houses, certainly, there is need for healing. Albeit, what kind of healing is being addressed? Is it educational, emotional, ethical, faith, financial, moral, motivational, physical, righteous and/or social? Whatever your needs are, seek God. See James 5:13-16. Verse 15 promises: *"And the prayer of faith shall save the sick, and the LORD shall raise him up; and if he have committed sins, they shall be forgiven him."*

Preachers' Kids: Living in Glass Houses are often stereo-typed as being Preachy like their Parents and/or Grandparents. Nevertheless, I thank God for giving us Saving Grace, Faith and Mercy in every area of our lives. Thank God for my loving kind and protective Parents. Thank God for their being *"an example of the believers,"* in Christ Jesus. My sincere prayer is that God will help us to always honor our Parents and their Godly bequest of Ministry to us. Let's examine what is happening in your life? We have many good and precious promises from the LORD. He will give you your heart's desire if you will commit your way unto Him and trust Him. Psalm 37:3-5 advises us to: *"Trust in the LORD, and do good; so shall thou dwell in the land, and verily thou shall be fed. Delight thyself also in the LORD; and He shall give thee the desires of thine heart. Commit thy way unto the LORD; trust also in Him; and He shall bring it to pass."* Amen. Amen.

Are you harboring any unforgiveness in your heart? If so, ask God for His forgiveness of yourself, as well as for others. Often times, I am asked these questions:

Question 1. How did you make it?

Question 2. How can I help my children to make it?

Answer: It was by the Grace of God and the application of His Holy Word.

We are Preachers' Kids: Living in Glass Houses, while hurting. Negativity may be churning within your heart because of wanton criticisms, and other things done to you by a few Church folk. As I thought on it, I came to realize that they may have been critical simply because they do not understand the culture of being Children of the Reverend Clergy. So let us stop the mind chatter as much as we can through prayer and supplication. You know who you are in Christ. You are the offspring of The Reverend Clergy. So ask God to save you from your yourself. Ask Him to save you from people. Pray and ask God to save you from the sin of unforgiveness.

Continuing our trek, we have arrived at Chapter 18: The Life of Preachers' Kids. What a blessing from the LORD to be the posterity of those who Serve and Minister the Gospel of Jesus Christ to the people. Living a life of righteousness is not always glamorous, but having the favor of God on ones life is a blessing. We can never take for granted our bequest. Yes, from time to time, we do desire to feel special. Yet, God has given our lives a special Ministerial assignment. We are the Offspring of The Reverend Clergy. Albeit, we are not pleased that our lives tend to be forever on display. Another expectation of us is to act as walking Bibles. If we do something people feel we shouldn't, we are referred to as the "worst kind." We are the worst kind of what? Accusations hurt, but there are also many happy times. Although we do not always see the glamour, but God has chosen us, the posterity of His Servants, for such a time as this. No more complaining. Amen. Amen.

Reverend Clergy, you may have been ever busy helping Parishioners and others. Yet, you seldom spend quality time with your Family. When will it end? Try to adjust before it is too late. Children grow up fast. So endeavor to give them memories of an active Ministry, also dedicated to Family living. God has called you to preach His Word, but not at the expense of your Family. I invite all of us to celebrate the lives we have been given. Embrace the Family business [Ministry]. It is time to strengthen the Preachers' Kids alliance. Let us continue to grow from strength to strength.

We have traveled together, in ecstatic concert to Chapter 19: Children of The Reverend Clergy. We are the Children of those who serve. Be encouraged! Know that the gift of Ministry is an amazing mission. Thus, I speak ministerial blessings over you and yours. Acknowledge that Ministry is a declaration to how much we are loved by God. It is not a burden. We have been chosen to the service of others, because He knew that in Christ, we could do it. Be resolute and allow your efforts to bring Glory and Honor to God, in Christ Jesus. *"For we are labourers together with God: ye are God's husbandry, ye are God's building."* (I Corinthians 3:9) From time to time, negative words may be spewed out by Opining Anesthetizers designed to numb and/or hinder you. Neither poisonous words, nor vicious acts can prevent God's divine call on our lives. Some people may profess to love you, but their actions may differ. Beloved, I am writing to remind you that God loves you perpetually more! His unadulterated Word says so! Amen. Amen.

God never make mistakes. When He made you, He knew your end from your beginning. Thus, let's agree with Psalm 139:14. *"I will praise Thee; for I am fearfully and wonderfully made: marvellous are Thy works; and that my soul knoweth right well."* You are important to God. He is acquainted with all your ways. Let's rejoice in praises to Almighty God. We are the apple of God's eye. Hence, pay no attention to inquiring Anesthetizers. When a person tells you that you are a mistake and a good for nothing, simply ignore it. Do not get caught up in pointless negative rhetoric. Let people know that you are here by the Grace of God. Beloved, that's enough! You are the Righteousness of God in Christ Jesus. So it is time for us to reclaim our God-given heritage. It was bequest to us by The Reverend Clergy, servants of our Lord Jesus Christ.

In synchronizing our journeying experience, we have arrived at Chapter 20: From This Day Forth. The time is now for no more dishonest excuses. Excuses can take on the perception of glorified reality. When you recognize that things are not as they seem, cancel that false scenario. We have come out of hiding in Lodebar. The feast had been prepared in the presence of our enemies. All the plots and plans of the enemy has been canceled. Hallelujah!!

While Jesus was hanging on the Cross at the place called Calvary, where they crucified Him, He said, *"It is finished."* What is finished? Everything He was sent to this earth to do was complete. He fulfilled His Father's will for mankind by shedding His Blood. Our Lord and Savior, Jesus Christ suffered, bled and died that we might live the abundant life. His "Mission Accomplished" gave us the right to the tree of life. So cancel negativity that people have spoken over your life. Put your trust in the Living God. When faced with adversity of any kind, resist the devil and he will flee. Remember Acts 20:24: *"But none of these things move me, . . . so that I might finish my course with joy, and the ministry, which I have received of the Lord Jesus, to testify the gospel of the grace of God."* No problem can break you unless you sign for it. In essence, if you do not make the problem yours, it will not impact you.

Continuing with our travels, we have journeyed from one chapter to another. Presently, we are at Chapter 21: Words of Encouragement by Bishop Joseph P. Bowens. Here, we are admonished to renew our minds with the Word of God. He cautions us to change our way of thinking. Know that Words have power. Practice using positive faith-filled words as we travel through life. Replace ugly thoughts with truth, honesty, purity, justice, love, virtue and things praise worthy. Today, there is a battle going on in the minds of men, women, boys and girls.

Simply, ask the LORD to renew your mind. God has the last say. He specializes in things that seem to be impossible. You have been hanging out with chickens in the chicken coup. Every time you make an attempt to fly; you are faced with negativity. You have been told that your dreams will not work. So stop hanging out with chickens. Did you know that you are an EAGLE? It's time for you to throw the chickens some chicken feed. It is high time for us to soar on wings of EAGLES. God will enable us to reach transcendent heights in Him.

These encouraging words of wisdom were given to us by my brother and Pastor, Bishop Joseph P. Bowens. He advised us to: ASK The LORD to RISE UP! RISE UP! RISE UP! Hear the voice of Your people. Show Yourself strong on our behalf in every facet of our lives. Thank You LORD, in advance, for showing Yourself strong. We Love and Honor You. To God be the Glory! Amen.

"In every thing give thanks: for this is the will of God in Christ Jesus concerning you." (1 Thessalonians 5:18)

In Summary: What an awe-inspiring tour. Finally, we are here at Chapter 22. Epilogue: Merging the Trek. We journeyed from one chapter to the next, while making our way through twenty-one exalting chapters. At long last we are arriving at the finale. During this visit, the trek is blended and merged into: In Summary. Our travels began with the *title* Preachers' Kids: Living In Glass Houses. After journeying through the Front Matter, we continued our motif with Chapter One. Our Only Wish Is To Be Normal. From there, we trek forward, chapter after chapter, lifting up the lives of all those who serve humanity. Together, we have made our way through the Table of Contents' rundown. As we synchronize and finalize our amazing tour, we must include our resources: A Useful Study Reference. Most importantly, we must stop and give An Offering of Praise Unto the LORD. For without Him, writing this book would have been impossible. In closing, the Benediction is given from II John 3, 4. At this point, we conclude our End Matter with:

- "May the Lord Bless You"
- Contact Information
- About the Author
- Coming Soon: Other Inspirational Books!

"For God is my witness, whom I serve with my spirit in the gospel of His Son, that without ceasing I make mention of you always in my prayers; Making request, if by any means now at length I might have a prosperous journey by the will of God to come unto you." (Romans 1:9-10)

ASK: The Key to Answered Prayer

See Matthew 7:7-8

Ask, Seek, Knock

ASK   "Ask, and it shall be given you;

SEEK   Seek, and ye shall find;

KNOCK Knock, and it shall be opened unto you: For every one that asketh receiveth; and he that seeketh findeth; and to him that knocketh it shall be opened."

                                                Amen. Amen.

A Useful Study Reference

Bible Verses Cited

"Feeding the Hungry Souls"
II Kings 7:1-20
Matthew 25:35-36

Welcome
Proverbs 10:22
Psalm 34:8

Acknowledgments
Matthew 19:14
Psalm 68:1

A Prayer of Thanks
Psalm 34:3

Chapter One
Luke 22:54c-60a
Proverbs 22:1
Psalm 25:2
Psalm 19:14

Chapter Two
John 10:10

Chapter Three
John 5:1-15
Proverbs 6:31
II Corinthians 10:12, 18

Chapter Four
Psalm 99:12

Bible Verses Cited

Chapter Five
Jeremiah 29:11
Job 3:25
John 8:32, 36
I Peter 5:7
Matthew 18:18-20
I Corinthians 2:9
Luke 11:1b, 4
Matthew 5:12
Matthew 6:14-15

Chapter Six
Psalm 118:24
Psalm 119:133-134
Hebrews 13:5-6
Psalm 37:23
Isaiah 40:31
John 8:36
Galatians 5:1
I Samuel 30:8
Luke 11:1-4
Micah 6:8
Philippians 4:6
Matthew 19:26b
Ecclesiastes 3:1-8

Bible Verses Cited

Chapter Seven
Nehemiah 1:1-11; 6:1-4
Ephesians 6:12
II Corinthians 10:4
II Corinthians 2:11
John 10:10
Nehemiah 8:10d
Psalm 101:7
Proverbs 6:16-19
I Peter 5:8
Luke 4:4-10
Ephesians 6:12
Matthew 6:33
James 4:7
Hebrews 1:2-3
Mark 14:38
Proverbs 10:22

Chapter Eight
John 10:10
Matthew 12:37
Romans 12:1-2
Philippians 2:5
Galatians 5:16
James 4:6
I Peter 5:5
I John 2:15-17
Proverbs 8:13
Ephesians 2:10
Isaiah 43:18-21
II Corinthians 5:17
Psalm 51:10-12, 14-15
Luke 18:13c

Bible Verses Cited

Chapter Eight (cont'd.)
Hebrews 4:16
Isaiah 43:25-26
Jeremiah 30:17a
Matthew 15:26
James 5:15
Exodus 23:25

Chapter Nine
I Corinthians 3:9
Job 22:28
Matthew 12:37
Proverbs 18:21
Psalm 101
Luke 23:34a
Psalm 118:24
Philippians 3:13-14
Proverbs 3:5-6
II Corinthians 10:5
Jude 20
Galatians 6:7
Romans 10:3; 12:3
I Corinthians 3:21, 23
I Corinthians 4:7
II Corinthians 10:5
Philippians 2:3
Philippians 3:18-19
I Timothy 3:6
II Timothy 3:2-5
James 1:17
James 2:9
Matthews 13:23

Bible Verses Cited

Chapter Ten
Job 22:28
Philippians 4:19
Revelations 3:20
Matthews 11:28
Joel 2:25-26
Luke 15:11-32

Chapter Eleven
John 10:10
I Peter 5:7
Ecclesiastes 3:1
Titus 3:12-14
I Peter 5:8
Psalm 23:1, 4
Proverbs 18:21
Matthew 18:19
Psalm 150:6
Exodus 3:13-14
Isaiah 50:7
Joel 2:25-26
Psalm 46:10
Proverbs 31:26-28
James 1:5
Proverbs 4:22-25
Ephesians 6:12
Proverbs 4:26-27
II Timothy 1:7
Galatians 3:13
Hebrews 4:12, 14
Hebrews 12:2
Romans 8:28
I Peter 5:7

Bible Verses Cited

Chapter Eleven (cont'd.)
Proverbs 23:7a
Philippians 4:8
II Corinthians 10:5
Matthew 6:14-15
Isaiah 43:25-26
Romans 12:2
Isaiah 43:18-19
Psalm 43:5
Philippians 4:8
Hebrews 13:6
James 4:7-8a
Proverbs 4:7

Chapter Twelve
Jeremiah 9:23-24
Psalm 23:1
Isaiah 26:3-4
Romans 12:13
Jeremiah 1:5, 8
Matthew 25:40
Leviticus 20:7
James 1:19-20
Proverbs 18:13
I Thessalonians 4:11-12
Proverbs 10:19
John 5:2-9
Matthew 9:37-38
I Timothy 6:6-8
Exodus 20:12
Galatians 5:22-23
Hebrews 10:23

Bible Verses Cited

Chapter Thirteen
Revelations 3:8
John 15:16
Philippians 1:6
Proverbs 10:22
Isaiah 43:18-19
Psalm 23:5
I Corinthians 2:9
Isaiah 55:11
Psalm 91:10-11
Psalm 34:7
I Peter 2:24
Matthew 8:16-17
Isaiah 53:4-5
Romans 8:2
II Corinthians 10:3-4
Ephesians 6:11
Ephesians 6:16-17
Psalm 91:1
Psalm 112:7
Exodus 15:26
Deuteronomy 32:39
Psalm 90:1-2

Chapter Fourteen
Matthew 6:33
II Timothy 2:15
Galatians 5:7
Psalm 46:10
Psalm 115:14-15
II Corinthians 2:11
John 10:10
Proverbs 18:22

Bible Verses Cited

Chapter Fourteen (cont'd.)
Genesis 2:24
Joel 2:25-26
Psalm 23:4b; 27:1
II Timothy 1:7
II Corinthians 10:5
Luke 9:11
Matthew 6:33
Psalm 119:105

Chapter Fifteen
I Peter 5:7
Philippians 4:8
Isaiah 49:15c-16
II Timothy 1:7
Psalm 23:4, 6
Hebrews 13:5-6
Psalm 27:1
II Timothy 1:7
I John 4:18
II Corinthians 10:5
Luke 9:10a, 11
Matthew 6:33
Psalm 27
Habakkuk 2:1-4
II Thessalonians 5:18
II Corinthians 1:20
Ephesians 1:18

Chapter Sixteen
I Kings 19:11-12
Isaiah 30:15
Ephesians 6:12

Bible Verses Cited

Chapter Sixteen (cont'd.)
II Corinthians 10:12
Psalm 139
Matthew 6:33
Psalm 127:3-5
I Peter 5:7

Chapter Seventeen
James 5:16b
Ephesians 2:10

Chapter Eighteen
I Timothy 3:5
Luke 15:11-24
Jeremiah 3:14, 22
Psalm 84:7
Mark 16:15
II Samuel 22:28
Psalm 31:20; 59:12; 62:9
Psalm 101:5; 131:1; 138:6
Proverbs 8:13; 11:2
Proverbs 16:18-19
Proverbs 18:12; 20:6
Proverbs 21:24; 30:12
Ecclesiastes 6:2; 7:8; 18:2
Matthew 10:39
Isaiah 64:6
Matthew 9:13

Chapter Nineteen
James 3:5-10
Genesis 6:3
Proverbs 18:21a

Bible Verses Cited

Chapter Twenty
Genesis 9
Amos 9:13-15

Chapter Twenty-One
Philippians 4:8
Romans 12:1-2
Numbers 10:35b

Chapter Twenty-Two
Psalm 46:10
Galatians 5:22-23
I Corinthians 13:13
John 15:13
I John 4:16
Isaiah 6:8
Colossians 3:16
Philippians 2:16
James 5:13-16
Psalm 37:3-5
I Corinthians 3:9
Psalm 139:14
Acts 20:24
I Thessalonians 5:18
II John 3, 4
Romans 1:9-10
Matthew 7:7-8

An Offering Unto The LORD
Psalm 118:23-24
Proverbs 10:22
Proverbs 3:9-10
Psalm 68:11

Bible Verses Cited

The Benediction
II John 3, 4

May the Lord Bless You
Numbers 6:24-26

Contact Information
Proverbs **10:22**

Bible Verses Cited

Coming Soon!
"More Inspirational Books"
Thessalonians 5:16-18

About the Author
Romans 1:16-17

An Offering Unto the LORD

"This is the LORD's doing; it is marvellous in our eyes. This is the day which the LORD hath made; we will rejoice and be glad in it." (Psalm 118:23-24)

LORD, I Honor You with the Firstfruits of this Book. Use this Offering for Your Glory. Bless Your People and all Humanity in accordant to Proverbs 10:22. Amen.

"Honour the LORD with thy substance, and with the firstfruits of all thine increase: So shall thy barns be filled with plenty, and thy presses shall burst out with new wine." (Proverbs 3:9-10)

Being called by God to Ministry, I am not ashamed to tell men, women, boys and girls about the Lordship of Jesus Christ. Where people are hurting and/or facing trials and challenges, I am willing to pray for them, anyplace and at anytime. Amen.

"The Lord gave the word: great was the company of those that published it." (Psalm 68:11)

The Benediction

"Grace be with you, mercy, and peace, from God the Father, and from the Lord Jesus Christ, the Son of the Father, in truth and love. I rejoiced greatly that I found of thy children walking in truth, as we have received a commandment from the Father." (II John 3, 4)

"May the Lord Bless You"

"The Lord bless thee, and keep thee:

The Lord make His face shine upon thee, and be gracious unto thee:

The Lord lift up His countenance upon thee, and give thee peace."

-Numbers 6:24-26

Preachers' Kids:

Living in Glass Houses

Contact Information

Need Prayer?

Want more information, or for
Book Signings, Speaking Engagements,
Fundraising, et cetera; please
write, call or email:

Rev. Dr. Arnetha Bowens

ABM Media

P.O. Box 777
Hanover, MD 21076

Phone: (843) 212-4264

Email: arnetha.bowens@gmail.com

May God Bless You!!!

*"The blessing of the Lord, it maketh rich,
and He addeth no sorrow with it."*
—Proverbs 10:22

Coming Soon!!

TWO BRAND NEW BOOKS

by

Rev. Dr. Arnetha Bowens

RESPECT

The Missing Ingredient

Respect IS Free NOT Cheap

"LET'S PRAY"

An Inspirational Scripture-based Prayer Book

"Rejoice evermore.
Pray without ceasing.
In every thing give thanks:
for this is the will of God in Christ Jesus
concerning you."

I Thessalonians 5:16-18

About the Author

ARNETHA BOWENS is the eighth child of Bishop George Law Bowens, Jr. and Mother Mary Ruth Bowens. [May God Bless Their Memory] She is a daughter of South Carolina: the Palmetto State. She is a true Southern Belle. Arnetha is continuing her Parents Ministry Legacy: "Feeding the Hungry Souls Outreach Ministry for Christ" on WJAY Radio 1280 AM, Mullins, South Carolina. She is on Radio every Sunday afternoon at four o'clock. She can also be heard every second Sunday morning on the Smith/Cooper Program at 9:30 a.m. It is indeed an honor and a privilege having been bequeathed this sacred opportunity. The joy of walking and working in her Parents founding tradition is a treasured blessing.

Desiring to make a difference, in the lives of fellow PKs and the Children of those who serve, prompted her to write this book. Arnetha loves people. She has a compassionate concern for mankind. Her desire to bring joy, encouragement and motivation to others, whenever and wherever possible. As a Communications' Specialist, she is taking the love of God to hurting people every where. Arnetha loves the Lord with all her heart. She is not ashamed to tell men, women, boys, girls about the Lordship of Jesus Christ. When people are experiencing difficulties, she will pray for them, and with them anytime and anywhere.

Reverend Doctor Bowens is a consecrated Evangelist. She is a Pulpit Teacher/Preacher and a Motivational Speaker. Listen to her weekly Radio/Television Broadcasts. In addition to her WJAY Radio Ministry, she is currently on Spirit 1400 AM Baltimore: "Real Talk" every Monday from 12 Noon to One o'clock p.m. Rev. Dr. Bowens is a regular on The Word Network with Bishop Michael Jones. Her Internet presence can be heard on Spreaker.com. Follow her on Facebook and the Internet. Attend her classroom seminars, workshops and discussion groups. *"For I am not ashamed of the gospel of Christ: for it is the power of God unto salvation to every one that believeth; to the Jew first, and also to the Greek. For therein is the righteousness of God revealed from faith to faith: as it is written, THE JUST SHALL LIVE BY FAITH."* (Romans 1:16-17)